REFUGEE
MINISTRY
in the Local Congregation

To
my son, Shawn P. Mummert

—*J. Ronald Mummert*

La and Chanh La Vanh and H'Ben Cabbage,
from whom I have received
more than I have given.

—*Jeff Bach*

REFUGEE MINISTRY

in the Local Congregation

J. Ronald Mummert
with Jeff Bach

Dover Memorial Library
Gardner-Webb University
P.O. Box 836
Boiling Springs, N.C. 28017

HERALD PRESS
Scottdale, Pennsylvania
Waterloo, Ontario

BV
4466
.M86
1992

Library of Congress Cataloging-in-Publication Data
Mummert, John Ronald, 1941-
    Refugee ministry in the local congregation / by John Ronald
Mummert with Jeff Bach.
        p.   cm.
    Includes bibliographical references.
    ISBN 0-8361-3580-6 (alk. paper)
    1. Church work with refugees. 2. Antelope Park Church of the
Brethren (Lincoln, Neb.) 3. Lincoln (Neb.)—Church history.
I. Bach, Jeff, 1958- . II. Title.
BV4466.M86 1992
259'.08'694—dc20   91-42220
                                                                CIP

The paper used in this publication is recycled and meets the mini-
mum requirements of American National Standard for Information
Sciences—Permanence of Paper for Printed Library Materials, ANSI
Z39.48-1984.

REFUGEE MINISTRY IN THE LOCAL CONGREGATION
Copyright © 1992 by Herald Press, Scottdale, Pa. 15683
    Published simultaneously in Canada by Herald Press,
    Waterloo, Ont. N2L 6H7. All rights reserved.
Library of Congress Catalog Number: 91-42220
International Standard Book Number: 0-8361-3580-6
Printed in the United States of America
Cover and book design by Paula M. Johnson

1 2 3 4 5 6 7 8 9 10 98 97 96 95 94 93 92

Table of Contents

Foreword

The ministry of a local congregation depends on many factors. A key one is coming to see ministry as an integral part of Christian living. Often congregations are led into ministry by the creative imagination and dedication of a core group of committed persons. These faithful visionaries draw others into outreach and service, which multiplies the blessings—and may change the spiritual tone of the entire group.

I have seen the blessings and frustrations of congregations committed to assisting in resettlement of refugees. In my experience, congregational sponsorship can be the best model of refugee resettlement. In the United States, resettlement is not implemented by the government; it is carried out by private agencies (with government support and monitoring). The government is sometimes involved, but citizen participation is key. This is why congregational involvement is so needed.

The authors define *refugee* as "a person without a home and in exile, needing help." That definition is appropriate, given this book's focus on resettlement's human face. It can help congregations keep human factors paramount amidst the challenges of refugee work.

It is also important to recognize the intricacies of resettlement. These are evident in the United Nations' more technical definition of refugee and in the fact that, when governments make decisions concerning who is a refugee or allowed into a country for resettlement, complex political and social factors are involved.

As congregations explore the complexities of the refugee issue, they will recognize that resettlement in a distant, foreign land should be a last resort. Concern for refugees thus includes working to change political and economic imbalances so refugees can be repatriated to their homelands or need not flee in the first place.

Congregations should also realize that, because of serious political and human shortcomings, not all refugees are recognized as such by governments. The sanctuary movement and Overground Railroad are examples of networks responding to unrecognized refugees. These networks rely on congregations to go outside normal channels in ministry to refugees. Undocumented refugees face not only the same trauma as those arriving through government channels, but also the trauma of uncertain status. This book can be a valuable tool in addressing such needs as well.

During the years I worked with Mennonite Central Committee (a relief, service, and advocacy agency) facilitating resettlement ministries, I met many unsung heroes of ministry to newcomers. This book offers an extended example of such outreach. The authors share many insights that can help others entering this ministry, as well as those struggling to work through difficulties of refugee work in which they are already engaged.

An expression of the authors' philosophy of ministry is embedded in their phrase "when a congregation and refugees minister to each other." Key to quality refugee resettlement is this realization that refugees may have as much to offer us as we have to offer them. As the authors note, meeting refugees raises the question not only of

"Who are you?" but also, "Who are we?" If evangelism is defined as gaining a deeper understanding of the good news of God's work in the world, such insight can come from startling directions. God uses the weak and humble to teach the strong and self-satisfied.

Refugees and sponsors almost always have different agendas that will clash at some points and merge at others. Indeed, refugee sponsorship can bring changes into the congregation which trigger reactions and needs in the lives of the sponsor. These sponsor needs can lead to growth or withdrawal.

For congregations who choose involvement in refugee ministry, I offer this encouragement: your efforts will be rewarded. This will be so even if your outreach does not lead to the extended program this book describes, or to mutual understandings culminating in refugees accepting the faith precious to you and joining your church.

In many cases refugees will move away, not accept your advice, appear to go behind your back, follow paths you do not approve. But despite the difficulties, and regardless of the extent of your involvement with refugees, the ministry will be worthwhile. Use this book as a key resource (along with others available from resettlement agencies)—and plunge in!

—Donald M. Sensenig, Director, 1979-1990
Immigration and Refugee Program
Mennonite Central Committee, U.S.

Acknowledgments

Many persons helped in the preparation of this book, above all Jeff Bach. Although I am primarily responsible for the content of the book, Jeff helped me with the details and mechanics of the writing at every step of the way.

My thanks to Bethany Theological Seminary in Oakbrook, Illinois, as well as to Warren Groff and Estella Horning, who contributed suggestions to improve the original manuscript for my doctor of ministry dissertation.

My thanks also to the following persons who contributed valuable insights to this work in many different ways: Many Kim, Ken Lohrentz, Lew Champ, Donnita Payne-Hostetler, Marvin Hostetler, Edward Kolbe, Mel Luechens, Sam Weber-Han, Cindy Weber-Han, Naomi Fast, Bruce Hankee, Tim Lanham, Woodrow Choate, Hugh Stone, Stacey Carpe, Tim Button-Harrison, Eath Oum, Rabbi Ethan Seidel, Earl Harris, Floyd Bantz, Norlyn Driver-Davis, Donna Duerr, and to the many refugees at Antelope Park Church of Lincoln, Nebraska.

Special thanks to Shawn P. Mummert for typing the manuscript on computer disk and to my editor, Michael A. King.

—*John Ronald Mummert*
Des Moines, Iowa

Introduction

I served in ministry at Antelope Park Church of the Brethren in Lincoln, Nebraska, for five years. One significant outreach of the church was ministry with refugees from various countries, mostly from Cambodia.

Under the Witness Commission of the Church Board, a small group of individuals interested in refugee ministry at Antelope Park Church became the Khmer Interest Group. On May 8, 1987, the group decided to sponsor a family of eight persons. The story which then unfolded inspired this book.

Refugee Ministry in the Local Congregation has evolved from material intended to address and facilitate that specific ministry in a book designed to help guide any congregation's intentional and international refugee ministry. My thesis is that the program for refugee ministry employed at Antelope Park Church of the Brethren can serve as a model for other churches or groups considering refugee sponsorship and ministry.

We define *refugee* as a person without a home and in exile, needing help. However, to help a refugee, we need some concept of the needs, the feelings, the stark realities which are part of being a refugee. Often refugees come out of a background of years of warfare. They leave homes and country in crowded ships destined for nowhere, only to arrive at crowded refugee camps where food is inadequate and health is threatened. After a long wait, they arrive in host countries to begin a new life.

This wrenching experience requires sensitive listening before we engage in other necessary tasks of refugee ministry.

Thus in chapter 1, the experiences of just such a Khmer refugee are shared. Many Kim's story was typical of some two hundred Cambodian (Khmers) who came to Lincoln, Nebraska, under the sponsorship of numerous churches and agencies.

Key elements discussed in chapter 2 include (1) empathy for refugee families who arrive in a strange country and have survived only at great personal sacrifice; (2) the process by which a congregation chooses to become involved in refugee ministry to serve displaced humanity; and (3) a brief history of the Antelope Park Church's ministry to refugees.

A Biblical Framework for Refugee Ministry is presented in chapter 3. From the beginning, refugee ministry at Antelope Park Church was seen as a spiritual ministry to the newcomers. The spiritual aspect of refugee ministry is a key consideration in developing an adequate vision for ministry. Biblical passages and stories, with their many descriptions and visions of proper care for sojourners and exiles, are consulted.

Chapter 4 focuses on the reasons for individual involvement in refugee ministry at the Antelope Park Church, according to research data gathered from members of the church when the congregation evaluated its refugee program. The chapter basically answers the question of why persons or a church become involved in refugee ministry. The research suggested these answers: 1. call from God, 2. service (mission perspective), 3. individual/congregational past experience, 4. humanitarian need, 5. personal experience, 6. available resources, 7. leadership/professional involvement in resettling agencies, 8. an intentional church decision to minister to refugees, 9. listening to the personal stories of the refugees, and 10. evangelism—sharing the faith with others.

The experience of refugees is one of fleeing a threatening situation in their previous home area for the promised safety of a new place. That new place may be quite similar to or radically different from their own culture. While no two experiences are alike, many refugees may have rather similar stories, despite the differences in specific details.

Obviously the refugee experience cannot be reduced to a simple three-step progression such as the phases of entry, assimilation, and accommodation presented in chapters 5, 6, and 7. Yet these phases help summarize the experiences of refugees and the needs that accompany each stage. To that end, the discussion in chapters 5, 6, and 7 highlights some dimensions of the initial entry of refugees into a new culture, the process of adjusting to that culture and, finally, settling into a new life and setting.

By orienting to these three phases, congregations can prepare themselves to be aware of the needs of refugee ministry and can begin to take steps to respond to those needs—always aware that involvement in refugee ministry means receiving from the refugees as well as giving to them.

1

The Refugee Story of Many Kim

Before 1975, my family lived very comfortably, in peace and freedom. Then Pol Pot's troops invaded Phnom Penh and our peaceful existence ended.

On April 17, 1975, the Khmer Rouge terrorized my entire homeland by forcing all the people who lived in Phnom Penh to leave their homes for the countryside. The Khmer Rouge soldiers said we would be away from our homes for three days. Three days became a week. A week stretched into a month, then many months. Finally came the crushing news that we could never return to Phnom Penh—to go home meant death. We were forced to migrate to Prektachore, Kandal Province (the birthplace of my mother, Seak Kep). The road was crowded beyond belief, making travel difficult on the eight-mile journey by foot from Phnom Penh to our new village.

On the way to Prektachore, my family was delayed in the village of Kah Brak for one month. While we were there, several relatives of my brother-in-law informed the village leader that he had worked for the Lon Nol regime. These were the leaders overthrown by Pol Pot, who was now terrorizing us. The village leader, Bror Dhen Phoum, interrogated us about my family's activities before 1975. During the interrogation, the Khmer Rouge wrote down everything we said.

Frightened, my brother-in-law discussed the matter with my brother. They decided we should leave Kah Brak. Immediately, we left for Prektachore, where we lived for two years.

In December 1975, my brother and his family were separated from the rest of our family and forced to live with his wife's parents. In 1976 my brother-in-law and twelve other men were ordered by the local Khmer Rouge leader to go to another village. They were to help with the planting of rice for only two weeks.

My sister thought this might be a trap, since most of the people in the village knew that my father and brother had been soldiers during the Lon Nol regime and that my brother-in-law had been a professor of music. Both these occupations had fallen out of favor.

Before my brother-in-law could leave for the other village, however, the nurse diagnosed him as having cholera. His wife—my sister—also had cholera. After they recovered, my fourteen-year-old sister contracted the disease. It started with vomiting and diarrhea at 9:00 the evening she became ill. By 4:00 the next morning, she was dead.

The next day, cholera struck me. I first felt sick in the same hour that my sister died. A soldier who lived across the river from our house came to help me. He was also the village nurse. To save my life, he had to put intravenous medication in my arm. The next morning, two people took me in a canoe to the hospital, which was a three-hour trip. I did recover, but then flu and high fever kept me in the hospital for two additional weeks.

In the first years at Prektachore, my family and many other evacuees suffered grave discrimination. The other villagers looked down on us because we were from Phnom Penh. Often leaving us on the brink of starvation, they ate almost all the available food. They told us that if the rice crop grew well in the next year, we would not face hunger again. But that was a polite lie.

Life during this time was very, very hard. We did not have enough food to eat; we were all hungry. Out of desperation we ate food we had never eaten before, which made people even sicker. Some people died of hunger; many others were killed by the Khmer Rouge for having worked for the Lon Nol regime.

The Khmer Rouge leaders separated the people of the village into three groups. Those of us who had been moved there from Phnom Penh were called "April 17 People," named for the date of our evacuation.

People who had lived in the village a long time, but who had relatives from Phnom Penh, were called "Triem," which means "to wait for." This group had a better life than the April 17 People.

People who had been born and raised in Prektachore and lived there all their lives were named "Pen Ceet." They were offered the opportunity to do many things—even to become village leaders.

My thirteen-year-old sister, Mara, was separated from our family and forced to join the "youth group." Even I was separated from my family. They forced me to go with the "small children's group." At least our group and the youth group were given porridge to eat. The women's groups were given no porridge, receiving only two bananas and half of a *kvet* (a bitter fruit the size of an orange).

Continuing to suffer many physical problems, the oppressed people's lives did not improve, despite the better rice crop the next year. Sometimes the village leaders continued to withhold food. Because no medicine was available, many people in the area died.

Separated from my mother, I lived in a big house with the small children's group. One night at 2:00 a.m., my leader awakened all of us. We were to go to the river and unload a boat full of rice plants. Still partly asleep and confused, I thought a crack in the house wall was a ladder. Stepping into the hole, I fell. [Such houses in Cambodia are often built on platforms, necessitating ladders.] I was unconscious for twenty-four hours. When I woke, I saw a friend sitting beside me. My friend had brought some medicine which was used to heal me following the accident.

Before my accident, the small children's group had been notified that we were to be moved to Takan Province, a place far from the village where our family was located. Two of my relatives had already been sent there. When I recovered from my fall, I was told to go to Takan Province to join the rest of the group.

My sister Malis met me there. She was very sick. One leader from our village secretly helped my sister escape death. The leader told her that if the Head Leader asked her what hospital she wanted to go to, she must answer that she wanted to go back to our village; however, if she said she wanted to go to a hospital, she would be killed. When the Head Leader asked Malis which hospital she wanted to go to, Malis chose to go back to the village of Prektachore. So, accompanied by the leader who had assisted her, my sister went back to Prektachore.

On January 17, 1979, (during my convalescence) Vietnamese soldiers arrived in our area and took control. Some people ran into the jungle to hide. Others went back to their homes. No one knew what to expect. My sister-in-law and I were allowed to return to Prektachore, along with others who used to live there. It took us about two weeks to walk from Takan Province to our home in Prektachore.

We found that everything in our home had been taken. Malis was still very sick and could do nothing. Because neither of us could do anything, our family did not get much rice. Only Mara and three others (my sister-in-law and her brother and sister) got some rice.

Many people from Prektachore, most of whom were men, had been killed during the years of the Khmer Rouge reign. Villagers who were ethnic Chinese or Vietnamese had also been killed, along with their whole families, by order of the government. Even three-day-old babies were killed. Because our house had been close to the island where they took people for execution, we could hear them if they cried loudly or shouted during their killings.

Six weeks later, we broke into the common kitchen to get rice, sugar, salt, fish—anything there might be to eat. We wished to cook in our own home as we did before 1975, rather than in the communal kitchens. (When the Khmer Rouge came to power, they had told us to bring together all of our food, so that everyone could share a common kitchen. Cooks would prepare the food for the working people.)

After we had taken the food from the common kitchen, we cooked it and shared it. All the people who ate with us were very happy because they could eat together as families again. They said that the food was delicious. Instead of having to take what was given to them, as was the case during life under the Khmer Rouge, they were able to choose what they wanted to eat.

The people in our village decided that a group would go to Phnom Penh to get the things the village needed. When they returned, some people had started to build a new house. They were not yet finished when some Khmer Rouge soldiers came back to our village. Since we had received word that they were coming, we ran back toward Phnom Penh so they could not find us. We were one or two villages away before they arrived.

A man and a woman in our village acted very strangely; they did not run away with us. The Khmer Rouge soldiers dug a hole in the ground. Leaving only their heads above ground, they forced the man and woman to climb down in the hole and buried them. They cried out for help, but no one was allowed to help them. They cried until they died. When we returned to the village, they were still buried in the hole—dead.

After the soldiers had left and we returned to our village, some of my friends and I decided to go along with the people who were going out to the island where the Khmer Rouge soldiers had killed people. Some people found necklaces, rings, bracelets, earrings—all made of gold. Some people found gold in the shirt pockets of the dead; sometimes gold items were found beneath bodies, or even hanging on trees.

When the people had come to the island, they did not know they would die. They brought their money and gold with them. When they discovered they would die there, they had tried to hide or even throw away their money or gold, trying everything to keep their valuables from going to the soldiers or the leaders. The soldiers and leaders investigated to see if the people hid their gold or money. They said that everyone must be honest to *Anka* (the government). If the soldiers learned someone was hiding valuables, they punished the person.

After the Khmer Rouge were gone, we lived in Prektachore for about two years, but in 1981 we moved back to Phnom Penh. Our house had been damaged. However, there were many houses which had been owned by people who were killed, so we could live in any vacant house that did not belong to the government.

On Wednesday, September 19, 1983, five of us left our house early in the morning and went to the bus station. We had decided to leave Cambodia. My two older sisters and my niece stayed behind. When neighbors asked where we had gone, my sister told them that we were going to visit some of our cousins in Battambang Province. When we arrived at Battambang, we were separated from one another. My mother, my nephew, my brother-in-law, my brother-in-law's mother, and I each went to different houses in different sections of town.

Because I had lighter skin, the guide said I had to remain at Battambang. [A guide was a person paid to lead people trying to flee the country.] I stayed there for nine days, waiting for the rest of my relatives to arrive. After they came, all of us stayed together in one house for only twenty-four hours. The next day we left at sunset.

We did not take any of our belongings with us when we left. The guides said they would bring our belongings to us but never did. As soon as the sun had set, we ran across the street and up into the mountain. Then we waited until 9:00 that night.

Two Vietnamese soldiers came and led us to a place called Seng Sanhah. On part of this journey, we had to ride in a canoe; we then walked through the water for the rest of the night. We had not eaten any supper before we started the journey, but the Vietnamese soldiers gave each of us a piece of cake to eat.

After we reached a house, the people who lived there cooked rice for us. We were too tired to eat, but we could not even sit down to rest because as we started to climb up the ladder in the house, we saw flashlights coming toward us. The guides whispered that we needed to get away immediately. So we continued walking in the water. We were very silent, careful not even to whisper.

Once out of sight of the house, we came out of the water and hid with one of the guides in the forest. The other guide went back to the house where we had stopped; he said he would be back soon. He did not come back for a long time. While he was gone, we saw a flashlight shining and realized someone was trying to find us. He stopped near us and coughed, trying to give a sign that we would answer. We wanted to call out to him in case it was Naim, the guide who had left us. The other guide very softly said that if it was Naim, he would know where to find us without our calling. We later learned that the man searching for us was a robber.

Naim returned in the morning. We left our hiding place in the forest and walked on a narrow road lined with thorn bushes. Since the road was very muddy, walking was difficult. Finally we reached the border of Thailand and Cambodia. The border area was controlled by Khmer soldiers. A Khmer soldier saw us and took us to his camp. The commander of the camp was Nong Chan, the man controlling the refugees who fled to this area.

Nong Chan demanded that we pay him 3,000 *bath* (equal to $150). We said we did not have any gold or money with us, but Nong Chan accused us of lying. He knew we were a rich family, he said. Why were we complaining when we had so much money?

We said we were telling the truth: we had no money. But Nong Chan still did not believe us. If we did not bring him the money or gold, he would send us to prison and have us searched.

We tried to bargain with him. Not wanting him to know we did have some hidden gold, my eldest sister told Nong Chan that if he would take us to the next refugee camp, we might be able to borrow some money from our relatives. Nong Chan agreed. He allowed his soldiers to take us to the next refugee camp, not far away.

Thinking all the refugees from Phnom Penh were rich, most of the soldiers in the border areas were like robbers. The soldiers often shot escaping refugees, then stole their valuables. Many people were killed along the border as they tried to escape the Vietnamese rule, just as we were doing. We were fortunate that these soldiers had brought us to their leader.

It was extremely dangerous along the border between Thailand and Cambodia. If we did not meet Khmer robbers, there was always danger from Vietnamese or Thai soldiers. Three different times we avoided being stopped by soldiers who would have killed us or stolen our money.

We stayed in the second camp for seven days, resting from our tiring journey. We began to feel better. My older sister made a plan for us to go to Khao I Dang Camp. The guides told her it would cost the equivalent of $4000 for each person to go, even for the little baby. They said they would give her a lower price if she could find some more people to travel with us. My sister asked her acquaintances; twelve of them decided to go. Soon we had thirty people. With the guides, our group totaled almost forty.

A week after we arrived at the second camp, we left. At 4:00 that afternoon we ran out into the jungle, one by one, hoping no one would see us. We walked along the road, never using a shortcut. We waited in the jungle until 9:00 p.m. before crossing the small river marking the boundary between Thailand and Cambodia.

There were three babies with us. As we were crossing the river, one baby began to cry; then the other babies began. Their crying seemed very loud in the still night. Suddenly Thai soldiers opened fire on us with a mortar and two machine guns. Our group scattered. The mortar was firing in the direction of the crying babies. When the mortar fell silent, there was no more sound of crying.

During the shooting, I saw one of the women in our group fall down in the grass. I thought she had been hit. I cried out and ran toward her. My older sister also ran to her, but the woman was not hurt at all. When the machine guns stopped firing, my sister and I began to walk, not knowing what direction to take. In the silence, we heard the Thai soldiers coming to look for us. The soldiers stayed on the road, but we had scattered into the jungle. When they had passed us, we began to walk on the road again. Soon we were joined by my brother-in-law's mother.

Wandering in aimless confusion for most of the night, we would move ahead and then look back. Around 3:00 in the morning, we came upon one of the guides with my eldest sister and a man from our group who had hidden under a small tree during the shooting. The guide had long hair and was kneeling so close to the ground that I almost stepped on him before I saw him. Thinking he was a ghost, I was so terrified I almost shouted.

He pulled me to the ground quickly, covered my mouth, and whispered to me who he was; I calmed down a little. We were hiding in a place close to the soldiers' camp.

About 4:30 that morning, the guide said we would have to find our way back to the camp on our own. Thai soldiers with flashlights came by on patrol. Whenever they turned away from us, we would crawl on the ground like babies. We were close to the soldiers, but because we crawled so quietly, they did not hear us. We found the river again and crossed back into Cambodia.

After dawn, we continued walking back along the road we had traveled the night before. The guide told us to wait for him under a certain tree. He said he would come back and bring the soldiers to escort us. We waited and waited, but he never returned—instead, soldiers with guns came and ordered us to come with them.

After the soldiers arrived, my sister got away. The rest of us ran as well, but we did not know where to go. Two members of our group hid where the soldiers could not find them and got away. The soldiers ordered the rest of us to follow them back to camp.

While we were walking, one of them said forty people had left the night before, but his leader responded that only twenty had gone. My mother begged the soldier to allow us to go home. She offered to give each of the soldiers the equivalent $200. One soldier seemed agreeable, but the leader of the patrol would not allow it.

About a mile from where I had seen my sister had run, I saw her running in the jungle. A soldier shot at her, but in the wrong direction. He called out for her to stop, but my sister just kept running as fast as she could.

The soldiers brought us to a large, thatched hut, where they treated us like dogs, accusing us of being enemies. They said we were not thinking about our country or anything but ourselves. I hated them for this. I would not look them in the face. I even refused to eat the food they offered us.

The soldiers called each of us in to meet with them. They asked each one of us why we wanted to go to Khao I Dang Camp. I was the last one they questioned. I told them we had to go to visit our brother there, because we missed him so much.

They continued the interrogation. Finally, because of my anger, I refused to look into their faces and told them, "I never want to see you again!"

The soldier asked me, "Why don't you answer the truth? Don't you know that escaping is dangerous? You are still young. Why don't you answer with the truth?"

I implored him to believe me. I promised I would not try to run away again and begged him to believe that I was telling the truth.

Reeking of too much wine, the commander came very close to my face. "If you don't tell the truth," he said, "we will shoot you." He waved his gun at me.

When my mother saw this, a pained look came into

her eyes, and she began to cry. I knew she was afraid they would shoot me.

"What are you crying for?" they asked her. "Do you want to eat this gun yourself and have its bullets in your head, too?"

My mother kept on crying. Just then the soldier who had first brought us there came and gave the officer the equivalent of $2,000 to free us, so he could take us back to our house.

Those of us who had been interrogated were reunited, except for my sister. My niece thought my sister—her mother—was dead or being held prisoner. She cried endlessly and refused to eat.

Three days later, the guides came back from Khao I Dang Camp. Some of the original group of forty had made it there! They brought photographs of those in our group who had made it. There was no picture of my sister. Nobody in our family believed she was still alive.

When the guides tried to assure us she was alive, we asked why they did not bring her picture. One of them answered that she was staying with her father-in-law in the camp, but we still wanted to make sure she was alive. Two days later, when the guides were in our camp again, we decided to try to go to Khao I Dang Camp.

On November 25, 1983, we did reach the camp. I still do not know how we managed. The camp was surrounded by three rows of fencing, so it was difficult to get inside. The night was dark, and the air frigid. While we were searching for the gate, we found some robbers sleeping on the ground outside the fence. They were covered with warm blankets. When we saw them, we were so frightened we felt as if our souls would leave us.

We were lucky. Continuing to sleep, the robbers gave us no trouble.

By 3:30 a.m., we had climbed the mountain and walked halfway down the other side. The guides had us wait there in hiding while they arranged for us to enter the camp. When the guides came back, they brought a soldier who had been guarding the fence. He led us through the gate. Once inside, we ran from block to block, from section to section, until we found the part of the camp where we were supposed to go.

We were considered illegal refugees in the camp from the day we arrived. We were not reclassified until August 28, 1984. Everyone who came to the Khao I Dang Camp after June 1982, was classified as an illegal refugee by the Thai government, which meant they would not take care of us. They gave us no food or water. Even housing was restricted to legal refugees.

My family had a hard time. Having no relatives in a third country (a country other than our place of origin or Thailand, where the camp was located), we had no one to supply us with money to buy rice and other essentials. The rice in the camp was expensive, and the price went higher every day, as more and more people came into the camp. We became very hungry.

Because we had paid the guides to lead us to the camp, there was very little money left after the journey from Cambodia. We had purchased just a little rice, which we used to make porridge. My family shared this porridge among ourselves. There was only enough for one small bowl per person. We tried to save as much of our money as possible, in case we were not reclassified.

The hunger was bad enough, but the biggest problem

was the periodic searching of the Thai soldiers for illegal refugees. They were always trying new methods to catch us and send us back to the dangerous border area.

My mother's cousin, who had been living in the camp since 1982, was a legal refugee. He and his family helped us hide from the soldiers. When my mother's cousin knew the soldiers were searching, he would come to our hut and warn us.

The distance between families within the camp walls was one-half mile. Our kind neighbors offered helpful advice. They told us to dig a very deep hole in the ground under the bed in our hut, to hide in when the soldiers came.

One day we were preparing food for lunch when the soldiers came. Our neighbors ran inside the hut and told us the soldiers were making a search. We climbed down into the hole and covered the top to hide from the soldiers. Our neighbor took the food away and also took the baby for us. When the soldiers came by, they saw nothing in the hut and kept on going.

The situation grew worse. We had to hide from the soldiers nearly every day. But our neighbors helped us keep away from them. They gave us hiding places when the night searches were made. They also gave us food, water, and some clothes. Whenever there was danger, we could stay with them.

The soldiers were not our only worry—at night we also had to hide from the robbers. The robbers came almost every night, but we could hear them coming because of the commotion they created.

On August 28, 1984, the Thai government declared that all refugees who had entered the country through that day would be reclassified as legal refugees. Now we came under the control of the United Nations High Commission on Refugees (UNHCR), which gave us food, water, clothing, and shelter. But we still did not have the right to be interviewed for exit to countries other than Thailand or Cambodia.

The people in our camp were divided into three classifications. One classification was KD, which meant one could remain in the camp and interview with any embassy representative. The classification we fell into was FC (family card), which meant that, though we could remain in the camp, we could not leave the camp or interview for exit visas. The third category was illegal refugee. Everyone who came after August 28, 1984, was considered illegal.

Now it was our turn to help the illegal refugees who got into the camp, just as we had been helped. We put aside some rice and sardines from our meals, giving this to the poor people classified as illegal refugees. Some people in the camp sold their sardines and rice, but we gave ours to the illegal refugees.

Since the robbers were afraid of becoming ill, the camp hospital and the area next to it (called Section 3) were the safest places. Some people, including us, would go there at night to sleep, so we would not be disturbed by the robbers. Then we would go back to our huts in the morning.

We were unprepared for the awful day which came unexpectedly upon us. My family and I had gone to Section 3 to sleep. Since I was not feeling well and felt hot in my chest, I could not sleep well. Around 4:00 a.m., I began to open my eyes sporadically. I awakened three of my neighbors and told them I was going home since I wanted to bathe, hoping to cool off. They came with me.

As we were walking through the camp in the early morning, we saw many soldiers out marching around the camp. They marched in groups, from block to block. This was unusual so early in the morning. My neighbors and I wondered about this. One of my neighbors said that perhaps an important visitor was coming to the camp.

By 5:00 a.m., I was home, and my neighbors went to their huts, about two blocks away. Suddenly, loud, patriotic music came over the loudspeakers. When the music was finished, a man's voice came over the loudspeakers, commanding everyone to stay in their huts. Wondering what was happening, most people appeared worried.

My sister and another neighbor had not gone to Section 3 to sleep the night before. I told them about the soldiers we had seen. My sister was suspicious and wondered why I had not called all our family to come home with me. I told her I had spoken with them, but they had wanted to stay where they were.

Around 6:00 a.m., the loudspeaker again carried the man's voice. Everyone was ordered to take out their KD or FC cards and line up in front of their huts. Now we knew what was happening—they were going to search for illegal refugees. My sister, my brother-in-law, and I were the only ones in our hut at that time. Our papers were with the rest of our family in Section 3. We went outside the hut empty-handed.

We waited a long time, but no one came to our section. We went back to our hut and started to cook a big pot of rice. My sister thought we should prepare some to give to the people hiding in the hole under our bed. It would be a long time until they could come out.

When the soldiers came, we left our hut. We knew the soldiers would take us to the administration zone since we did not have our papers. The soldiers did not go inside our hut. If they came upon one that was vacant, they went inside and searched it thoroughly, looking everywhere they could to find illegal refugees.

The soldiers asked for our papers. We said we had none, so they took us to the administration zone. There we saw many people with no papers, and many with inadequate documentation. Families were standing together in groups. When my mother saw us, she showed the soldiers the papers for us (which included picture identification cards). We were released immediately and permitted to go back to our hut. The soldiers caught thousands of illegal refugees that day. Some of them had been caught in bed, while they were still sleeping. Often people did not go to bed until late, because it was very hot, and they were afraid of robbers.

On September 29, 1985, all the illegal refugees in the camp at that time were reclassified. A voice came on the loudspeaker, calling everyone without papers to come to the administration zone to be documented. When the people gathered for documenting, the soldiers surrounded them to prevent newly arriving refugees from receiving legal status. Refugees entering the camp just one hour after the announcement could not go to the administration zone to be legally documented. With legal status, everyone with papers was now officially permitted to live inside the camp.

On January 1, 1986, we had a very happy day. My family was among those called up to be classified KD. Now we would be permitted to go out of the camp with soldier escorts to interview for exit visas to other countries. People who had siblings, parents, or spouses in the United States were called first to meet in the American embassy, but my family did not have relatives in the United States.

One day representatives from the Japanese embassy came to interview applicants. One did not need relatives in Japan to qualify for immigration, but the Japanese embassy was only choosing people with one to five members in the family. However, our group had been separated into two families when we were reclassified KD. We applied for exit visas with the Japanese embassy. On September 25, 1986, the Japanese embassy called us to meet with them. We were granted permission to emigrate to Japan. They took our pictures to show that we had passed the interview.

On October 4, 1986, the American embassy called our two family groups to meet with them. The American embassy had a four-step interview process: registration, then three classifications (JVA, EAO, INS). On the first day, we passed through three of these stages. Then we had to wait for INS (Immigration and Naturalization Service) to decide whether or not we could go to the United States.

On October 10, 1986, we passed our final interview with the American embassy. We passed because my father had been a soldier helpful to the American forces before 1975. Many people who had sisters and brothers in the United States were rejected by the American embassy. Only very rarely were people with no relatives living in the United States passed through all four steps of the emigration process. Usually, these were families who had worked for the U.S. government or soldiers before 1975.

On November 10, 1986, we left the camp to go to Pananikron, where they put only people waiting for exits to third countries. We stayed there eighteen days, then we went to the Philippines. We lived in a refugee camp there, studying English language and American culture.

On May 7, 1987, we left the refugee camp. We went to Manila and waited for an airplane that would take us to the United States. On May 8, 1987, we arrived in Lincoln, Nebraska. Earl Harris was my sponsor. There were other church families who helped us to get acclimated to our new life.[1]

Refugee Ministry in a Contemporary Context

Influx of Cambodian (Khmer) Refugees

Since the late 1970s, over two hundred Cambodian (Khmer) refugees have come to Lincoln, Nebraska. Thousands of southeast Asian refugees have come to the United States. Most of these refugees could tell stories of suffering like Many Kim's. Untold numbers have died trying to find a better life. And the refugee story is repeated constantly with new faces in new places.

The Antelope Park Community Church of the Brethren in Lincoln, Nebraska, was one congregation among the many religious bodies that responded to the arriving Khmer refugees. Eventually Many Kim would find her place among them.

The congregation's involvement with Cambodian refugees came about indirectly through the work of a member, Mary Frazier. As a placement coordinator, she turned to the congregation (where her husband at the time was pastor) for assistance. As was stated in a denominational publication at the time,

> Glenn Frazier explained that the congregation "decided to be in spiritual ministry to the newcomers." With the help of

a small grant from the Church of the Brethren's Parish Ministries Commission, the congregation has set up leadership training classes, which in turn have bolstered their Bible studies.[1]

As a result, the ninety-seven Khmer refugees who came under the care of the Brethren nearly doubled the congregation's size.

Leadership training, growing Bible studies, and the outward signs of growth indicated only superficially the deeper sense of mission in the hearts of Antelope Park members. Ministry to the refugees meant, in many respects, starting all over. The story of this one congregation demonstrates the many issues involved when a congregation and refugees minister to each other.

Even after the members at Antelope Park had committed themselves to refugee ministry, they faced this question: who **are** these people? The answer continues to unfold in the telling and retelling of the stories of people like the Khmer and the Antelope Park congregation.

Telling the stories, which is the purpose of this book, begins to explain who refugees are. And defining refugees invites others to join the story of the challenge and joy of refugee ministry.

Definition of Refugee

Senator Alan K. Simpson of Wyoming confessed that even those like himself, who must discuss refugee relief in a government context, may have trouble with definitions.

> Let me tell you the toughest thing for me. The average American citizen and the average American congressman have no

concept of the difference between a refugee, an immigrant, an asylee, a permanent resident alien, or a special entrant. . . . [2]

The United States Committee for Refugees (USCR), in a comprehensive survey of public attitudes on refugees and immigrants, confirmed that Senator Simpson's assessment of public awareness is accurate.

> Fewer than half of those polled [750 adults from the full range of socioeconomic levels] can correctly explain the difference between refugees and immigrants, most are not aware of the relative magnitude of the numbers of refugees, legal immigrants and undocumented aliens entering the country, and there are widespread misconceptions as to the countries from which refugees come. Refugees, of course, are fleeing actual or likely persecution resulting from their race, religion, nationality or political beliefs or behavior. Immigrants enter the country for a variety of motives, most often family reunification or the desire for better economic opportunity; by definition, they enter the country legally. Undocumented aliens, usually referred to in the media as "illegal immigrants," do not have government permission to be in the United States; presumably their motives are mainly economic. [3]

Based on this survey information, it is reasonable to assume the average Christian does not know the difference either. The United Nations defines refugees as "people who have fled their own countries because of fear of persecution for reasons of race, religion, nationality, or membership of a particular social or political group."[4]

Elie Wiesel's definition turns common descriptions upside-down, turning the refugee into our judge:

So what is a refugee? Only someone who is a victim of an oppressive, inhuman society and, therefore, deserves our respect and perhaps our gratitude—surely our compassion. Think of refugee. Here is a man or woman or a child who arrives in a new place where he inspires suspicion. . . . So, these poor people who needed someone did not get accepted. . . . Somehow they were not adopted. . . . Why not? Imagine a refugee who comes to a new country where he has no friends, where everything is a burden. His language is a burden. . . . It means being a refugee may be a metaphysical condition, then, not only a political situation.

Strange again—when these people come into a new country. . . . In the new country everything is different—its geography, its science, its morality or certain concepts of morality. It is then that any refugee whom we confront becomes our judge. He passes judgment on our values, on our society.[5]

Yet a simpler definition is possible. A refugee is *an exile without a home who needs help*. A refugee is someone who must rely on someone else for aid in this predicament. To offer aid, however, helpers must have some concept of the needs, the feelings, the stark realities which are part of a refugee's experience.

Gretchen Sousa, a missionary in Mexico and later in Central America, describes refugees as "sojourners . . . fleeing from another pharaoh. Bayonets and bombs replace bow and arrow, but faces tight with silent sorrow haven't changed."[6]

Paul Tabori voices the sense of exile in "Song of Exile." His poem aches with the emptiness, the shrinking ego, the erased pride, the escape that is often worse than prison felt by the exile. He mourns the loneliness even amidst crowds, the unfulfillable longing for a home never again to be seen, the chronic sadness that clings forever to the exile.[7]

Survival: The Key Issue

Refugees themselves, however, are not concerned about definitions. Usually survival is their key concern. Refugees share a common fate when they arrive in a receiving country. Bruce Grant addresses the array of people who, for a variety of reasons, become refugees. Grant shows insight into the perspective of both the refugees and the natives of the receiving country.

> A refugee is an unwanted person. He or she makes a claim upon the humanity of others without always having much, or even anything sometimes, to give in return. If, after resettlement, a refugee works hard or is lucky and successful, he may be accused of taking the work or the luck from someone else. If he fails or becomes resentful or unhappy, he is thought to be ungrateful and a burden on the community. A refugee is especially unwanted by officials: his papers are rarely in order, his health is often suspect. . . .[8]

To the daily lives of refugees, repeated humiliation, fear, and sense of loss belong. Beverly Raphael expresses how these experiences make refugees unique people.

> Refugee populations are a special group. . . . Their home may be left intact or destroyed; their communities may be in the hands of enemies. . . . For the most part, they have faced extreme disaster stressors at many levels and on many occasions. They may have confronted death daily, including the violent and mutilating deaths of family and loved ones. Survival may seem to have been bought at an impossible price. . . .[9]

Melissa and Brent Ashabranner point out that a feeling of overwhelming vulnerability often arises from the up-rooted existence of refugees. This feeling can persist long after refugees have entered a receiving country.

> Refugees are the most vulnerable immigrants to this country because they have had to flee from their homeland with little more than the clothes they wore. They are cut off from family and friends with no way to communicate with them. They have lost their culture, of which language is such a vital part. In most cases they have spent long, hard months in refugee camps. Most vulnerable of all are refugee children who have left their country without their parents or who have lost them in the hazardous escape.[10]

Human Displacement: Global Problem, Local Challenge

Perhaps the most striking aspect of the refugee problem is its global scope. There are some twelve million refu-gees in the world today. Global displacement of persons has increased greatly in the three decades between 1960 and 1990. The seer in Ecclesiastes speaks to this issue of today when he observes,

> Then I looked again at all the injustice that goes on in this world. The oppressed were crying, and no one would help them. No one would help them because their oppressors had power on their side. (Eccl. 4:1 TEV)

To the church of Jesus Christ, millions of wandering refu-gees present a need and an opportunity for ministry. Congregations such as Antelope Park illustrate some ways to take "strangers in our midst" seriously. Refugee sponsorship has been a significant witness of churches in the Anabaptist tradition. But the record still shows room for improvement. A newsletter from the Brethren service center at New Windsor, Maryland, illustrated the overwhelming need in the mid-1980s.

> Refugee Sponsorship for the Church of the Brethren congregations in 1986 was almost triple the number of churches that sponsored in 1985. Forty-seven churches opened their hearts and arms in 1986 compared to seventeen in 1985. The Refugee Resettlement Program facilitated the resettlement of 429 "new Americans" within Brethren congregations and with other resettlement groups such as ethnic community organizations, individuals, relatives, and other church groups.[11]

In spite of efforts by many religious bodies, 1986 was a bleak year for most of the world's refugees. An article concerning the following issues complicating the situation of refugees appeared in a 1986 Brethren publication:

> The situation for most of the world's 11.7 million refugees in 1986 saw little progress and even deterioration. This is the inescapable thread running through the recently released *World Refugee Survey—1986 in Review*, observes Roger Winter, Director of the US Committee for Refugees. Among examples cited:
>
> - the lessening commitment of the US and other western countries to resettling Southeast Asia refugees.
>
> - "Fortress Europe" where restrictive laws were tightened to keep asylum seekers out.

- South Africa's erection of a fence not merely to keep Mozambican refugees out, but with a capacity to electrocute those who encounter it.[12]

Political changes in Eastern Europe and the Soviet Union, and the Persian Gulf War with its displacement of countless Kurdish refugees only added to these issues.

The world refugee problem is a terrible one which may even worsen as social, political, economic, and environmental upheavals continue. Thus the church needs to consider refugee ministry as a viable addition to congregational mission programs. Despite stories like that of Antelope Park, other persons like Many Kim suffer hunger, sickness, and violence. Their needs compel congregational responses of compassion and care.

Important to addressing the problem is communication. How can the church respond to the needs of refugees worldwide, unless the stories of refugees concerning their exile are heard? Their voices were heard when the Antelope Park congregation took in its first refugee family. The voices have become clearer for the members in Lincoln since then.

The story those voices tell is one of tears, laughter, helplessness, and hope. It is the story of changing methods and renewed traditions. Above all, it is a story of new beginnings through Christ.

New Beginnings at Antelope Park Church

As exiles to a new land find people with open hearts and build a new life, another chapter is added to the ongoing story of God's people. Sojourners, refugees, strangers, pilgrims are only half of the story. Those who care, who open their hearts and who share, materially, emotionally, and spiritually are the other half. Bridging the gap between the two, God's love brings them together.

The new beginnings of refugee ministry came to the Antelope Park Church in 1955, when it welcomed a German artist, Herbert Thomas, and his wife.[13] Church members who shared family activities and hospitality spoke highly of the good times they had together as they made new beginnings. Later, Mr. Thomas showed his appreciation to the church by painting a large mural in oils in the main foyer of the church, depicting Schwarzenau, Germany, the birthplace of the Church of the Brethren.

New beginnings came again to Antelope Park when political events of the late 1960s and the following decades brought Vietnamese and Cambodians to Lincoln. Again, the message of God to Moses in Leviticus 19 gave direction.

> When a stranger sojourns with you in your land, you shall not do him wrong. The stranger who sojourns with you shall be to you as the native among you, and you shall love him as yourself; for you were strangers in the land of Egypt: I am the Lord your God. (Lev. 19:33-34)

On the day before Thanksgiving in 1975, thirty-one Vietnamese refugees arrived in Lincoln. American hosts welcomed the Tran family with tears, hugs, and warm handshakes. The thirty-one made up an extended family of a grandfather, a grandmother, an aunt, three sons and their wives, seventeen grandchildren, and five other related adults. There was no common verbal language between the new arrivals and their greeting committee. But the language of the heart was spoken freely.

Caring persons from five small congregations of south-east Lincoln committed themselves to meet the needs of this large group. For the Antelope Park congregation, this included a "spiritual ministry to the newcomers," as former pastor Glenn Frazier stated. Harold Gesell, a former church member, described the mission as one of meeting a "spiritual need." Meeting such need included baptizing the refugees when appropriate in the months following their arrival.

Refugees undergo many adjustments which are sometimes perplexing. Their hosts may not understand the newcomers' responses. When refugees make decisions their hosts cannot understand, sponsors may respond critically. For example, several refugees in Lincoln chose to move to places with more familiar climates and better financial support. Some Antelope Park members wondered why the refugees left; others sent them on with God's blessing. Both groups of members faced the challenge of ministering to those who remained.

How does a congregation keep alive the vision of refugee ministry? For Antelope Park, the answer was closely related to the "why" of refugee ministry. To address the "why," as well as find vision and direction, members turned to the Bible. True to its Anabaptist heritage, the congregation found in Scripture both faith and practical models for refugee ministry. The story of God's people in the Bible formed a basis for the unfolding story of people reaching out to each other at Antelope Park.

The biblical epic of the exiles speaks often of sheltering the stranger (or foreigner), clothing the naked, discerning the neighbor, freeing captives, befriending prisoners and comforting the sick. Failing to respond to the needs of refugees would mark the church's failure to discern and minister to human needs. It would also mark the church's failure to respond in faith to the story of faith. There is a biblical mandate to love and care for the refugees in our midst (and hidden from our sight). To that mandate in the biblical story, we now turn.

3

A Biblical Framework for Refugee Ministry

Heavenly Father, it is through two of your most powerful lobbyists, Moses and Aaron, that the first immigration law for refugees was enacted, when the Pharaoh let your persecuted but chosen people leave the land of Egypt.

The first immigration law that you enacted for your chosen people in their new land was not to mistreat the aliens living in your land but to treat them as you would love yourselves. "Remember, you were once aliens in the land of Egypt: I am the Lord your God."

All of us are aliens on this earth, refugees seeking the eternal safety, happiness, and peace of your heavenly land. Let us be mindful that on this earthly pilgrimage we are all equal in your sight. In your eye there are among us no kings, no queens, no rich, no poor, no learned, no fools, no legal or illegal aliens, no refugees, no natives. On this journey, let us hold each other's hand, helping each other each day to take another step towards you.

For it is only when we travel as brothers and sisters that we can reach your home and there be forever your sons and daughters. Amen.[1]

This prayer by Anthony Bevilacqua reflects the strength of Scripture as a foundation for refugee ministry. The ancient stories depict God's people as refugees who themselves were instructed by God to respond to the dispossessed. Both the Old Testament and the New Testament are rich with references to *sojourners* and *strangers*, terms which describe persons who find themselves on the "outside" of the community of God's people for a variety of reasons.

A brief examination of these stories and passages provides a biblical framework for doing refugee ministry.

Thrust Out of Egypt

Before the Exodus from Egypt, as Jorge Laura-Braud observes:

> Abraham and his family risked leaving all behind so that in trust upon a co-pilgrim God they might learn to live by promise to travel light and to know fulfillment by becoming a blessing to the other peoples of the world (Gen. 12:1ff.). Following arrival at the promised land, God's call, protection and liberation would be recaptured in the memory of the pilgrim beginnings, "A wandering Aramean was our father . . ." (Deut. 26:5)[2]

The Exodus from Egypt, the event that gave birth to the Hebrews as God's chosen ones, is the story of a refugee people. Oppressed slaves of Pharaoh of Egypt, the Hebrews were set free after a series of terrifying plagues. The climax of the plagues was the death of the firstborn of their oppressors. The former slaves were "thrust out" (Exod. 12:39) so fast there was no time even for their bread to rise. Later, memorializing Israel's ancestors, the Passover meal and the unleavened bread became symbols commemorating freedom.

Following the defeat of the Egyptian army at the Red Sea (or Sea of Reeds), the escaped laborers journeyed into the Sinai wilderness. When Israel later remembered the events of this liberation and journey toward a new land, they saw God at work. They recalled their beginnings as a refugee people, freed by the actions of God. The biblical tradition remembers the God who "triumphed gloriously; the horse and his rider he has thrown into the sea" (Exod. 15:1-2).

Alexander Campbell describes the impact of these events upon the Hebrew people.

> Thus the Hebrews were saved on that day, a day never to be forgotten in the annals of Israelite history. This was the day and this was the event that ever after reminded Israel that God had chosen them and they were God's special people.[3]

On the journey through the wilderness, Israel encountered the God who freed them at Sinai. Their God provided for their needs and, according to the biblical confession, led them to a new land that had been promised to their wandering ancestors.

Whatever ethnic origins lie behind the people who eventually became Israel and their settlement in Palestine, the biblical tradition sees the Exodus events as intrinsic to Israel's status as God's chosen people.[4] They remembered their beginnings as refugees who escaped harsh labor under the kings of Egypt, were delivered, protected, and led by God in wondrous ways. Central to Israel's understanding of its "election" was the memory that they were a refugee people.

For You Were Sojourners in the Land of Egypt

Israel's status as a refugee people was woven into the laws they received from God when they came into the new land God had promised. The kindness (*hesed*) that God had shown the Hebrews in their refugee journey was to be shown and repeated to the refugees (or sojourners, strangers, from the word *gerim*) living among them in their new land. Joseph Blenkinsopp describes the interpretive nuances which affect a reading of these laws.

> The resident alien (*ger*) and the native born are legally on the same footing; the phrase "there shall be one law for the native and the *ger* who sojourns among you" occurs routinely wherever this category is the subject of [the priestly] legislation . . . (e.g., Exod. 12:49; Num. 9:14)
>
> . . . .From the earliest days of the settlement there existed a class of resident aliens (*gerim*). . . . A *ger* was a foreigner who resided more or less permanently in the land under the protection of a particular clan and as a client or protege of a tribal head.

Blenkinsopp goes on to stress that, though the *gerim* were at the bottom of their society's status pyramid and often exploited, a distinctive aspect of Israelite life was the determination to care for such people. He notes, "In the Deuteronomic law, for example, they are listed with the fatherless, widows, and unemployed clergy as in need of a wide range of assistance (Deut. 14:29; 24:19; 26:12-13, etc.)."[5]

The refugee experience was embedded in the many laws that prevented the oppression of foreigners living in Israel's territory: "You shall not oppress a stranger; you know the heart of a stranger, for you were strangers in the land of Egypt" (Exod. 23:9).

The ethical implications of the refugee experience were spelled out explicitly in laws dictating Israel's conduct toward refugee sojourners among them. During the harvest, Israelites were not to strip bare the fields, orchards, and vineyards. The Law commanded them to leave produce that fell to the ground or the corners of the fields for the sojourners (Lev. 19:9-10, Deut. 24:19-22). Food and clothing were to be given to the foreigner (Deut. 10:18). God's law established justice for aliens in employment and in other matters (Deut. 24:14, 17).

One primary law binding for both Israelite and foreigner alike provided for sharing a portion of the prescribed tithe with sojourners (along with widows, orphans, and Levites) and all those who had no guarantee to land (Lev. 24:22). R. K. Harrison describes the Hebrew law: "Whatever the cause of a brother's poverty, he is to be given the hospitality accorded to a stranger or alien, and not be allowed to die of starvation." [6] Leviticus 25:35-38 reads,

> And if your brother becomes poor, and cannot maintain himself with you, you shall maintain him; as a stranger and sojourner he shall live with you. Take no interest from him or increase, but fear your God; that your brother may live beside you. You shall not lend him your money at interest, nor give him your food for profit. I am the Lord your God who brought you forth out of the land of Egypt to give you the land of Canaan, and to be your God.

Even the great thanksgiving confession of Deuteronomy 26 recalled the refugee beginnings before the Exodus, as well as Israel's refugee experience after the liberation from Egypt. In remembering their ancestors as wandering Arameans and recalling the Exodus as God's act of freedom, Israel confessed faith in the God who rescued and cared for them when in danger and need. That faith called Israel to share the abundance of the Promised Land with other refugees as a sign of the omnipotence and joy of God's provision.

The Law commanded loving the sojourner and providing for the needs of refugees based on Israel's own experience of God's love of them as refugees (Deut. 10:19). The stranger was to be treated as native among them. The people of God were to love refugees as themselves. The people of Israel were never to forget that they, too, had been refugees (Lev. 19:33-34).

Why Have I Found Favor in Your Eyes?

The story of Ruth and Naomi illustrates the laws regarding kindness to foreigners. When envisioned as a story about refugees, the Book of Ruth takes on new depths of meaning.

Naomi and her husband, Elimelech, along with their sons, travel to Moab as refugees from the famine in Judah. After the loss of her blood relatives, Naomi resigns herself to the loss of her foreign daughters-in-law. She prepares to leave Moab and return to Judah. Her daughter-in-law Ruth refuses to accept Naomi's dismissal. Instead, Ruth renounces her own family, her own nationality, and her own homeland. She voluntarily becomes a refugee to remain with Naomi.

In Bethlehem, Ruth benefits from the laws that granted the gleanings of the fields to the sojourners and widows

(Lev. 19:9-10). Furthermore, Boaz kindly extends his protection and offers Ruth eating privileges with his workers. Boaz even instructs his workers to leave, on purpose, some grain in the field for Ruth. She rightfully wonders why Boaz has shown such favor, since she is a foreigner.

As a result of the duty of the next of kin to raise offspring for the dead and to exercise the right of redemption of family ground, Boaz and Ruth are married. Soon a son is born. Then, in a surprising twist, the women of Bethlehem praise Ruth, not Boaz, telling Naomi that Ruth is "more to you than seven sons."

Ruth voluntarily became a refugee (in Bethlehem), to show her great love for Naomi, who had become an endangered refugee (a widow with no family) in Moab. Boaz's kindness in many respects was a response to Ruth's original kindness to Naomi and to the dead (Ruth 2:11). Throughout, God is the provider to whom those in need turn for refuge.

Do Not Oppress the Alien

In the prophetic literature, the plight of refugees does not receive the attention it did in older strands of biblical tradition. Jeremiah does, however, mention sojourners (*gerim*) specifically in a positive context. Jeremiah warned his hearers not to wrong the alien so the coming fury of God's judgment could be averted (Jer. 7:6; 22:3). More importantly, if God's people practiced justice, perhaps they would be permitted to stay in their land, rather then becoming refugees again.

Justice for those who had no protection was a major concern for the prophets. John Tenhula speaks of the importance of justice to the people of God.

Justice, translated in the Jerusalem Bible as "integrity," means the wholeness of the created order that exists when all the parts are balanced with each other. Thus, justice is the opposite of aberration and estrangement. When justice reigns, all of God's children will be reconciled to each other because no one any longer regards them as "strangers and sojourners, but fellow citizens with the saints and members of the household of God" (Ephesians 2:19). To achieve justice we must advocate for justice in our society. The writer of Proverbs urges us to "Speak up for the people who cannot speak for themselves. Protect the rights of all who are helpless. Speak for them and be a righteous judge. Protect the rights of the poor and needy" (Proverbs 31:8-9).[7]

Carnegie Samuel Calian notes that the disparities addressed by these laws still exist today.

> The contrast between "haves" and "have-nots" is creating two different perceptions of reality. These differing perceptions are headed for a clash; how violent a clash can only be guessed. What will be the role of Christians living in a global village divided by "haves" and "have-nots"? If the Christian community, consisting of rich and poor, seeks to be responsible, we must be more than a pietistic group that exists primarily to provide spiritual nourishment for our own members. We cannot afford to leave . . . injustice unattended. The total Christian community should instead . . . be the cohesive catalyst in . . . bridging the gap between "haves" and "have-nots."[8]

Justice for foreigners among the Hebrew people seems a concern limited in the prophetic tradition mostly to Jeremiah and later to Ezekiel (again, as an explanation for why God's people became refugees, or exiles in Babylon). According to Edward J. Brady,

Both Jeremiah (22:1-3, 13, 15-16) and Isaiah (58:6-7) are quite clear that doing justice means being faithful to one's relationships to the poor, the needy, and the alien. In fact, the marginals of society are the scale on which the justice of the whole society is judged. When the poor and oppressed are exploited, then the whole society has no true relationship to Yahweh.[9]

Isaiah 58:7 mentions the "homeless poor" as the recipients of compassion when the proper observance of fasting is fulfilled. Perhaps the outside pressure from foreign military powers, and the inside seduction by foreign gods, made it more difficult to raise concern for foreigners living amidst the Israelites. Yet the broad concern for justice evident in many of the prophets (Isaiah, Jeremiah, Amos, Micah) would extend to the alien who lived among the Israelites.

The experience of the exile was a new refugee experience of sorts for Israel. The prophetic traditions differ in interpreting that experience. One strand looked forward to a return of the exiles to Judah; it interpreted that return as a second exodus to the Promised Land under God's direction. Jeremiah anticipated a time when God would "bring them back to the land which I gave to their fathers" (Jer. 30:3).

The book of Isaiah heralded the change in Israel's fortune with the call to "prepare the way of the Lord, make straight in the desert a highway for our God" (Isa. 40:3). Ezekiel envisioned a new temple that would again be filled with the glory of the Lord (Ezek. 42, 43).

In these and other passages, Israel's prophets longed for an end to their exile and a return to the land and covenant of God's promise. They were forced into exile by a variety of causes. Their exile was variously interpreted in prophetic traditions. Nevertheless, many of Israel's prophets announced a time when Israel would again find refuge with their God, in the land God had given.

Neither Jew nor Greek

At the time of Jesus and the early Christians, the careful restrictions of Jewish law concerning contact with Gentiles erected well-guarded walls keeping in the chosen and excluding the foreigners. These walls came crashing down when Paul asserted that

> there is neither Jew, nor Greek, there is neither slave or free, there is neither male nor female; for you are all one in Christ Jesus. And if you are Christ's, then you are Abraham's offspring, heirs according to promise. (Gal. 3:28-29)

The early Christians no longer accepted the narrow limits of the Pharisees which supported the division of Jews, God's chosen people, from the Gentiles. The walls crumbled with the spread of the Christian mission beyond Judaism. In Christ, those who "once were far off have been brought near," and Christ became the peace that made one people out of many (Eph. 2:13ff.).

With Paul's preaching Gentiles could no longer be considered foreigners, sojourners, or strangers (words carrying similarities to "refugee" in the Old Testament) in the Christian faith. Those who were in Christ, regardless of race or nationality or gender, were no longer "strangers to the covenants," but "fellow citizens . . . members of the household of God" (Eph. 2:12, 19; Rom. 3:28-31).

Being God's people could no longer be defined by ancestry. Instead, inclusion in the people of God was by faith in Christ (Gal. 3:6-9, 14). It was thus open to anyone of faith, regardless of nationality.

Of course, this change did not happen instantly. The New Testament is full of the tensions of working out this good news. When the writer of Luke-Acts later tried to tell the story of this process, the account of Peter's vision in Acts 10 became the pivotal point of opening the Christian mission to the Gentiles.

Then there are the stories of the unknown Hellenistic refugees of Acts 8:4ff. and 11:19ff., Paul's missionary work, and the collection for Jerusalem. They illustrate the good news of welcoming those who were formerly "foreigners" (Gentiles in the New Testament setting) into full citizenship among the people of God—the church.

This brought new implications for how Christians related to refugees. The ethical imperatives of the Old Testament law were redefined when Christianity broke out of its initial Jewish context and began to reach Gentiles. These developments were made concrete when economic conditions necessitated a collection among the Gentiles for the Christians in Jerusalem (1 Cor. 16:1-4; 2 Cor. 8 and 9; Rom. 15:25-27).

Ministry to those in need, regardless of racial or economic background, became all the more imperative as Christians opened the community of God's people to all on the basis of faith in Christ. Labels of race, gender, and economic status were subordinated to trust in the risen Christ. All who came to Christ sought refuge in God's grace and became fellow citizens in the new community of believers.

Unto the Least of These

The Gospel traditions include stories of people working

out the practical considerations of this community of Jewish and Gentile believers. Matthew tells stories of practicing this faith in the new community of discipleship. At least two stories from Matthew, the Gospel long beloved in the Anabaptist tradition, refer in particular to refugee outreach.

Matthew alone tells the parable of the last judgment (25:31-46), when the peoples of the world will be separated into "sheep" and "goats." Those on the right hand of the Son of Man will be welcomed into the kingdom prepared for them. Those on the left will be sent away to eternal punishment.

The basis for this division and judgment is one's response to Christ. The surprise in this parable, both to the reader and to the "sheep" and the "goats," is that Christ has been present in the needy persons. Those who inherit the kingdom are surprised to learn that as they served those in physical and spiritual need, they served Christ. Those who fail to inherit the kingdom are surprised that as they refused those in need, they also refused ministry to Christ.

Among the needy listed in this parable are strangers. Certainly this parable's aim is not solely to advocate refugee ministry. But the Old Testament imperatives for justice and hospitality to the stranger and foreigner are radicalized for the New Israel, Jesus' followers, whose Messiah is found among strangers.

Matthew goes one step further than the Old Testament. God's Messiah, the Son of Man who will judge the whole earth, is identified among the "homeless poor" (Isa. 58) to whom Christ's followers are to minister. As Christians welcome strangers, they welcome the Lord of their faith. Every ministry of compassion, especially to "the least," is a ministry to the Messiah. As God so often sided with the poor in the writings of the Law and the Prophets, now God's Messiah takes the side of the poor, the homeless, the hungry, the thirsty, the naked, the sick, and the prisoner. The Messiah becomes one of them.

This parable is surprisingly good news indeed: the followers of Jesus will find their Messiah among the needy. In serving those in need, the community of faith will serve its Lord. Matthew's words of judgment sound a warning to Jesus' followers about the danger of missing the opportunities to serve the Lord by refusing even "the least of these, my brethren [and sisters!]" (25:40).

There is another story from Matthew's Gospel which expresses the concern of the Old Testament for the sojourner and links it directly to the Lord of faith coming among us. It is the narrative of Jesus' birth in Matthew 1 and 2. This story of the magi, and Herod's outrage over the one born "king of the Jews" explains Joseph's flight to Egypt with the child and his mother.

Again, there is more theological weight to this story than a New Testament rationale for refugee ministry. But in telling the story of Jesus' refuge in Egypt and his family's return to Palestine, Matthew has emphasized and reinterpreted concepts fundamental to the faith story of the Old Testament. Israel's Savior, like Israel herself, was brought out of Egypt as a refugee under God's protection.

Like the later parable in Matthew 25, the infancy narrative tells the good news that the refugee Messiah is God-with-us, Immanuel. Ann Weems captures the urgency of the refugee Christ in her poem "The Refugees." It evokes images of that ancient family creeping in terror through "the wild and painful cold of the starless winter night."[10]

Jesus Was a Refugee

In remembering that its Lord was once a refugee, the early Christian community of Matthew's Gospel was reminded of at least two central truths. It remembered, not only the theological significance of the Exodus for the Old Testament people of God, but also the Old Testament imperative about ministering to the homeless. James Cogswell sees this as a major theme of the Gospel accounts of the ministry of Jesus.

> The Gospels attest that Jesus spent much of his life as one "uprooted." Born in a borrowed stable (Luke 2:7), the infant Jesus was taken by his family as a refugee into Egypt to escape the death threat of Herod (Matt. 2:13-15). Jesus spent his early ministry on the move, as one who had no place to lay his head (Matt. 8:20; Luke 9:58).[11]

Again, the focus of Matthew's stories is not simply on refugees, but both lead to a similar practical expression of their broader truths. The Christian community becomes the fulfillment of the people of God in the Old Testament. Israel had found refuge in Egypt and had also been led out of Egypt and cared for by God in the journey to Palestine. God's law called for the hospitality, compassion, and justice for refugees that God had shown God's own refugee people.

The New Testament people of God, the New Israel, is ruled by the Messiah who had also been a refugee in Egypt and was led out under God's protection. Even more than the old Israel, the new community was called to show compassion, justice, and hospitality to the homeless, to refugees, to the sojourners, because their own Lord, the Messiah, had been a refugee. In showing compassion to the "least of these," they ministered to Christ, their Lord.

Other Passages

Other New Testament passages provide biblical motivation for ministry to refugees. Luke's concern for the poor (Luke 6:21, 24) may be considered among the ethical impulses calling for response to the homeless foreigners. The letter of James stridently insists on equality, even priority, for the poor. Passages such as James 2:14-16 suggest that for James the outward expression of faith in ministry to those in need (who include refugees) was as crucial as faith itself.

These are only a few of the many New Testament passages of the good news about Jesus Christ which call followers to a life of discipleship every day. In that daily discipleship, the faithful will respond to the needs of others. Among those needs are those of the sojourner, the refugee. Believing and practicing the Christian faith requires compassion and response to those in need. Christian faith focuses on Christ, who was a refugee and who continues today to encounter disciples as a refugee.

Summary

The Christianity of the New Testament reflects a diverse gathering of communities. Despite that diversity, however, through their faith in Jesus as the Messiah Christians united to become a new people of God. Faith in Christ made this diverse group a new people, a counterpart to the Hebrews of the Old Testament who became God's covenanted people.

This New Israel was gathered around a Messiah who, like the old Israel, had been brought out of Egypt as a refugee. The new people of God likewise responded with compassion and justice to the needy.

The good news that Jesus is Messiah and Lord binds Christians to the startling surprise that their living Lord of faith is found and finds them among those most in need. As Jesus's followers express their faith by ministering to the homeless and the foreigner, they minister to the Lord of their faith, they choose places of privilege for themselves and reject those without privilege, they fail to serve their Lord. Paul K. Knitter describes his vision for the church when this good news is truly perceived.

> The stranger, the new face, the man with the turban or the woman of a different skin color, will no long appear to us as a threat or an adversary but as a partner and friend. We will come to feel that as long as there are strangers—persons we do not know—we really do not know ourselves. "Once the assumption that the stranger is inferior is shattered, then he is experienced as a stranger. And once you admit that you do not understand him, you are gradually forced to admit that you do not understand yourself." Gradually but with mounting urgency, we are realizing today that in order to answer the perennial question "Who am I?" we have to ask the question "Who are you?"[12]

Charles Keeley echoes Knitter's concern, placing the question in the context of the larger society.

To work on refugee issues, if we are the least bit serious,

confronts us, as religious reflection does, with some basic issues: Who are we? How do we treat our fellow human beings? How do we build societies that respect and encourage our humanity? [13]

The Scriptures of Christianity confess faith in a Savior and Lord who was a refugee and continues to encounter the faithful as a refugee. Indeed, faith in the Messiah makes believers aliens, pilgrims, and, yes, refugees, in this world. Like Israel, the church's faith compels it to give aid, compassion, and justice to all types of refugees.

4

Motivations for Congregational Refugee Ministry

Scripture forms a foundation for congregational ministry to refugees. However, members of a congregation may approach service to refugees for several reasons. Faithful and effective ministry requires attention to this variety of motivations as congregations assess why they might begin or continue helping refugees.

The case of one local congregation reveals several factors motivating members to aid those who have fled native countries. The words of members at the Antelope Park Church show that a congregation embarks on this ministry for various reasons.

Call from God

One important motivation for ministering to refugees is a sense of a "call from God." Members felt compelled to respond to refugees because of faith in God. Earl Harris said, "I had felt called by God to become involved."

"Our desire to be faithful to the great commission of Christ led us to be helpful in specific ways to refugees and their concerns," stated Glenn Frazier, pastor at the time the Khmer arrived. He continued, "My involvement began with . . . a challenge from the Scriptures. . . ."

Mary Frazier confessed, "I felt a calling from God to commit my life to serving my brothers and sisters."

According to John Doran, "We are called by Christ through the Scriptures to help the less fortunate."

Dianne Epp stated, "I believe that as followers of Christ it is our mandate to minister to the needs of our fellow-man, and that when we see others in need, we are called to do what we can to meet those needs."[1]

For these members, aiding refugees was a response grounded in a faith commitment and their understanding of the Bible. By responding to refugee needs, they felt they were answering a call from God and Scripture.

Service: A Mission Perspective

A recurring motivation among Antelope Park members was the potential for service offered by refugee ministry. Orientation toward service requires a church to be outwardly directed rather than inwardly directed. Outward direction implies an awareness of the needs of persons outside the congregation and a willingness to respond to those needs.

An inward direction implies preoccupation (frequently appropriate) with the needs of the people already in the congregation. Inward direction becomes problematic when, as too often happens, only the needs of persons in the in-group are nurtured.

Paul F. Knitter's observation reflects the fulfillment that attention to both inward and outward needs can accomplish. "To be true," Knitter says, "religion must foster not only individual, but societal wholeness."[2]

Many congregations today may focus first on individual wholeness, or an inward attention to the needs of those already within the group. Personal spiritual growth may focus on private devotion, Bible study, and worship. Some churches may even work at encouraging group identity and relationships within the group, but the energy is still directed primarily inward. Fewer congregations strive for a societal wholeness which develops a mission program to help and heal society as a whole.

Refugee ministry in the local church works simultaneously at individual growth *and* social wholeness. For example, one member may learn a few new words or a new language. Members and those invited through refugee ministry interact, experiencing firsthand the encounter with a new culture.

The Third World often meets and confronts the First World in the refugee ministry setting. Refugee ministry affords the congregation an opportunity to face global problems in a local setting. Such ministry can take steps to respond to global injustice through personal, practical involvements with victims of injustice.

The challenge to a congregation to reach outward beyond itself in global dimensions is summarized by Langdon Gilkey.

> If the meaning of men's lives is centered solely in their own achievements, these are too vulnerable to the twists and turns of history, and their lives will always teeter on the abyss of pointlessness and inertia. And if men's ultimate loyalty is centered in themselves, then the effect of their lives on others around them will be destruction of that community on which they all depend. Only in God is there an ultimate loyalty that does not breed injustice and cruelty, and a meaning from which nothing in heaven or on earth can separate us.[3]

Individual/Congregational Heritage

Naomi Fast became involved in the Khmer ministry at Antelope Park because of her interests and volunteer efforts with a variety of other international programs in the city of Lincoln since 1968. Naomi, however, spoke not only of personal past involvement. She spoke also of the church's past experience. "I was attending the Church of the Brethren, where involvement and assistance with resettling refugees from various places had been a vital part of the church ministry for over ten years."

A dentist in Lincoln involved in helping refugees stated, "My dental practice has involved more than five hundred Vietnamese, ten Poles, four Czechoslovakians, one Lebanese, a number of Iranians, two Russians, one Italian, one Peruvian, one Brazilian, one Mexican, one Jamaican, and many other nationalities."

Similarly, Glenn Frazier's earlier work with Vietnamese and Ethiopians paved the way for the church's later involvement with the Khmer.

The Antelope Park congregation had an established heritage of involvement with refugees. Those who helped with the Khmer could identify this new outreach as another chapter of their ongoing story. Individuals within the congregation could relate the new response to their own past involvement.

Refugee ministry became a way to help more recent members to share in the congregation's heritage. Congregations entering refugee ministry may establish a precedent or a new heritage. They may now identify themselves as churches who practice this type of ministry. But the congregation's past can also de-motivate churches from refugee ministry with those famous words: "We've never done this before." Congregations which begin refugee ministry face the unavoidable uncertainties accompanying new involvements.

Humanitarian Need

Mary Frazier felt a great need to respond to the refugees present in Lincoln, Nebraska. "By September 1982, there were easily 220-250 Khmer people involved in the [Khmer] Placement Program." The need of so many foreigners with no place to live captured her compassion.

While much of this country's population tried to put the Vietnam experience in the past, the suffering which it created kept intruding on the present. As one church member, William Unrau, observed, "The effects of the Vietnam War were highly dramatized in the religious news in general, and in denominational publications in particular. There was increasing discussion of the plight of Vietnam refugees following the withdrawal of United States Armed Forces from Vietnam."

Some members at Antelope Park saw refugee ministry as a way to respond to the immense suffering in the wake of that war.

Personal Experience

Personal awareness of the need for refugee ministry helps motivate a congregation to this type of ministry. Educating members concerning the plight of refugees is an important step. William Unrau alluded to this factor. "Our pastor, Glenn Frazier, and Mary joined a group of volunteers overseas to learn of the desperate needs of Cambodian refugees in Thailand firsthand. It was this experience of our pastor that inspired a vision of the Khmer ministry."

The style in which Glenn and Mary Frazier shared refugee needs with the Antelope Park congregation helped members feel they had experienced first-hand contact with refugees. This sense of personal involvement is important in motivating members to engage in refugee ministry. When congregations sense personal ties to the needs of refugees, they can more easily respond.

Available Resources

Refugee ministry demands a wealth of human and material resources. Yet that wealth can often spring from small beginnings. Glenn Frazier reflected, "My involvement began with . . . an awareness that we had the resources to meet the challenge of the great influx of refugees to Lincoln."

Human resources are important in ministering to refugees. The involvement of Keith Funk illustrates the need for and importance of human relationships in the spiritual activity of refugee ministry. Keith said, "Glenn asked me if I would be interested (along with Earl Harris and Harold Gesell) in working with some enthusiastic Cambodians in developing a Cambodian leaders Bible study."

The pastor played a key role in identifying and motivating those persons he thought could help meet the spiritual and physical needs of the Khmer population. Thus through personal involvement, as well as through sharing personal material resources, people became ministers to the refugees in many ways.

Leadership/Professional Involvement in Resettling Agencies

Mary Frazier had worked for Church World Service (CWS), an ecumenical cooperative service agency shared among several Christian denominations. One CWS ministry is refugee resettlement. In 1981 CWS dropped the grant for a state-wide refugee coordinator. Mary decided to direct a Khmer Placement Program in Lincoln under Catholic Social Service, one of the largest Christian social agencies in the United States.

Mary's husband, Glenn, had begun involvement in refugee resettlement in Nebraska with Vietnamese refugees in late 1975. At that time Antelope Park Church, along with congregations of other denominations, decided to sponsor an extended family, the Trans. Thus personal connections with relief agencies may provide a motivating linkage for a congregation to participate in aid to the displaced through refugee ministry.

An Intentional Church Decision to Minister to Refugees

The various motivations for doing refugee ministry illustrate how important it is for a congregation to decide *intentionally* to begin such a ministry. This decision will obviously engage conversation about the various reasons for serving refugees. A church which participates intentionally in refugee ministry must ask the entire congregation to wrestle with the challenge.

Dianne Epp observes, "When the initial question of the Antelope Park Church of the Brethren becoming involved in ministry to refugees was raised by our pastor, Glenn Frazier, I was chairperson of the Witness Commission. He raised the concern in our commission meeting. I presented it to the Church Board and encouraged them to act positively upon it."

Glenn Frazier commented, "We made, as a congregation, a faith decision to work with the spiritual needs of Cambodian refugees, to accept them into our congregation, to teach them, to help them respect their own culture. We cared for and baptized them after instruction."

Those discussions and the ultimate decision were shaped by the multiple motivations for responding to the refugees. In many cases, members became interested for more than one reason. But the final decision required assessing and weighing not only needs and motivations, but also resources for responding. The ministry began when the congregation counted the cost, ascertained motivations, and committed resources to serving those in need.

Listening to the Personal Stories of the Refugees: The Eath Oum Story

The Antelope Park congregation's commitment to refugee ministry steadily increased as members actually met and interacted personally with real refugees.

William Unrau wrote, "We listened to moving reports from the refugees." Learning the stories of the refugees further enriched these personal interactions.

It is crucial for the ministering congregation to listen to the stories of personal pilgrimages of pain, agony, torture and, in some cases, death of family members. One refugee, Eath Oum, moved Antelope Park with his own representative story. (Another refugee, Vanna Pel, translated.)

I was a truck driver for my city in Kampuchea [Cambodia] from 1969 to 1975. Then, on April 17, 1975, (New Year's Day) the Khmer Rouge took over the country and forced all Khmer people to live in the rural areas and become farmers. We lost our home, our land, and other property.

They forced us to work very hard, without enough food or water. Most of our people died for lack of food. Some were caught and killed. Others died of pneumonia, their bodies swollen because they did not get enough calories.

We had to work very hard in the fields, with oxen. If we did not work fast enough, we were punished by beating with whips or by being deprived of food. We worked day and night, and our food was only one mouthful of rice soup and maybe some vegetables that were either grown in the field or found growing wild.

Sometimes we had meat. Sometimes not. A few pounds served to feed a hundred people. Most people died because they just couldn't keep their bodies going. There was much suffering.

At that time they separated families. I am a married man with seven children, but my wife was forced to live apart from me, and my children were also separated from us. We were all scattered, and we had no way of knowing how the others were doing. They wanted to kill me.

Two of my sons, one thirteen and the other eighteen, died at Boeung Croe County. After losing the two children, I decided to move to another county called Snoeung, where life was a little better.

In 1979, the Vietnamese took over Kampuchea and my family was reunited. We decided to escape to Thailand to find a better life. The first place we stayed was Khao I Dang Camp. We were there for one year.

Then they moved us to Camp Poth, where we lived for seven months before going to a transit camp, where we stayed one week. Next we moved to the Philippines and were put in English classes for six months.

On May 11, 1983, we came to the United States. We were very pleased to find people who cared for us, supported us, and paid attention to us—especially the people from the church. It meant so much to us, and we shall never forget it as long as we live. Now we have a better life.[4]

The Evangelism Factor

The most controversial issue concerning refugee ministry at Antelope Park was the role of Christian evangelism. Harold Gesell, a former member, described one view of evangelism in Antelope Park's Khmer ministry. "Evangelism had a big role to play in the ministry to the Khmer. The people needed to be evangelized. Evangelism should have played a bigger role than it did. The language barrier was an obvious impediment to evangelism at the beginning of the ministry."

Dianne Epp saw evangelism from this perspective:

> Some of the Khmer people who settled in Lincoln already had been introduced to Christianity in the refugee camps. That is, they had already been introduced to "evangelism" and wanted to relate to the church because of that.
>
> I believe one of the dangers of refugee ministry is the use of material aid as a tool of evangelism. If we are called to meet the needs of all people, in so much as we can, then evangelism may follow. But it must in no way be a prerequisite or used as a manipulative device.

Dianne Epp's words echoed Andre Trocme's experience with Jewish refugees during World War II, as told by Philip Hallie.

Help must never be given for the sake of propaganda; help must be given only for the benefit of the people being helped, not for the benefit of some church or other organization that was doing the helping. The life and the integrity of the person helped were more precious than an organization. And so Trocme would never try to convert the Jewish refugees who came to Le Chambon, a small Protestant town in Southern France.[5]

Evangelism is a proper and necessary element of refugee ministry. But refugee ministry should never be used as an instant membership drive or reputation boost.

5

And You Welcomed Me: Entry

Although the Antelope Park Church of the Brethren had a history of relating to refugees over the years, many members felt unprepared for the wave of refugees and needs that came with the group of over forty Khmer. Congregations seeking to begin refugee ministry may have no background or preparation for such a ministry. Even settling one individual, let alone a family, can seem overwhelming without adequate preparation. Few persons or congregations can fully anticipate the needs arising from the arrival and settlement of refugees.

Church members often become aware of a refugee's needs through personal involvement. A congregation can begin to appreciate the tremendous suffering many refugees experience. Churches can experience great joy from welcoming persons from foreign cultures. In these respects, congregations are equipped for refugee ministry not only in preparing for it, but also in practicing it. Members of the Antelope Park Church have discovered there is no substitute for doing the ministry.

Antelope Park identified three stages in the life of new refugees which may benefit other congregations. The stages are named here as entry, assimilation, and accommodation, although other names could be used. Each stage involves preparations which can ease inherent difficulties that will arise. But a flexible understanding of the stages is also important, because each experience of refugee ministry will differ.

Just as the needs of refugees change during each stage, so too must the response of the congregation. This chapter describes practical ways congregations can prepare and engage in ministry to refugees entering a new culture. Chapters 6 and 7 suggest preparation for and practice of ministry during the stages of assimilation and accommodation. In dealing with each stage we describe clusters of needs under the following headings: physical, emotional, psychological, community, cultural-language, and spiritual.

Refugees entering a new culture bring a host of needs and generate others on arrival. Many needs, such as basic physical ones, are obvious. Emotional needs for love and friendship, as well as the psychological need to tell stories of past experiences and memories, may be obscured by language and cultural barriers. Refugees may have acquired some ideas about their new land while in refugee camps. Many of these ideas, however, may match actual experience as little as many American tourists prepare to understand a culture they will travel to visit.

Other needs, such as those resulting from the radical change in culture, will remain hidden until the two persons or groups can communicate across different cultures. Examples may be as simple as learning how to observe traffic signals or not playing in the streets.

Physical Needs

Housing

A first priority for resettling refugees is to locate housing for the individual or family, preferably near others of similar ethnic background. If this is not possible, having a support person, sponsor, or family from the congregation living near the refugee can be helpful. The quality of housing is important. Often refugee service agencies, either private or governmental, provide helpful resources.

Food

A congregation must plan to supply food to refugees until they can earn income to purchase food. Learning about types of foods that are part of the refugee's culture is important. North Americans may be surprised to learn that not everyone likes cheeseburgers, french fries, or pizza. Some people never learn to like them. As a wider variety of ethnic foods are available in American stores, food may not present as many problems as it did a few decades ago.

Not only are foods different, but methods of preparation differ as well. Congregations should not expect refugees to arrive knowing how to use appliances.

When preparing for dietary needs, the age and health of the refugees should be taken into account. Babies, children, and senior citizens will have needs that differ from other adults. Refugees who have suffered from malnutrition will need special attention to diet.

Clothing

Clothing will be needed until the refugees can make or

purchase their own. Depending on climatic and cultural differences between the native and host countries, the refugees may need to become accustomed to new ways of dressing. Some refugees will need to learn to wear things they have never worn and may not enjoy wearing. A North American moving to a sub-Saharan climate, for example, needs to adjust clothing preferences.

Of course, a variety of clothing sizes will need to be considered. Changing seasons require clothing appropriate for changing climate. Providing refugees with clothing is not an excuse to give someone what you would not wear yourself. Clothing is a personal expression; this should be considered so as not to diminish a person's dignity.

Medical Care

Some refugees arrive requiring immediate medical care. Others have medical conditions that need continuing care. Still others have undiagnosed health problems. Stephen Grenier, a physician and member of the Antelope Park Church, cautions that medical care concerns should not provide excuses for avoiding sponsorship of refugees.[1]

Congregations should plan in advance to provide medical and dental attention for refugees. Someone able to interpret is necessary for refugees seeking medical and dental care.

An immediate need for the refugee family is basic first-aid supplies and instructions on how to use them. Caution is necessary with medications. Someone must make sure refugees understand directions for dosage and consequences of overdoses.

Employment

Eventually a refugee will need employment to become self-supporting. Skill levels vary widely. An occupation common in the home country may be limited or nonexistent in the new society. Goatherding is seldom required in North America, for instance.

Language proficiency plays a role in employment. Jobs such as dishwashing, cooking, or domestic cleaning may be the only ones open until refugees get more training or develop better language skills.

Again, refugee service agencies may provide leads for employment. Refugees will need to provide the proper legal documents to employers, such as their I-94 ("green") card and Social Security numbers. Congregational members may be able to provide employment or suggest refugee employment leads.

Working with the System

In preparing for the physical needs of an arriving refugee it is vital for a member or committee to learn channels of assistance, documentation, and support that exist in government and private agencies. A refugee service center, for example, lists the following family support services:

FAMILY CASE MANAGEMENT: child/day care, immigration and naturalization service assistance, social security help, food, legal, translation, personal counseling, group counseling, housing, school, transportation.

EMPLOYMENT COUNSELING: college, drop-out, group counseling.

HEALTH/MENTAL HEALTH: crisis/emergency, counseling, social adjustment, translation, transportation, mental stress, relative abroad, health.

COMMUNITY EDUCATION: child/day care, housing, school, counseling, crisis emergency, legal, translation, transportation.

TRANSPORTATION/DRIVERS EDUCATION: driving education, job support transportation.

VOCATIONAL/EMPLOYMENT REFERRAL: vocational, employment.[2]

Denominational staff persons involved in refugee resettlement can be a first source for learning about these support channels. State agencies or local religious organizations can help teach the best use of the government bureaucratic structure. Refugees and their support people will be involved with bureaucratic processes for a long time. A necessary preparatory step is to learn who, what, and where the structures are and how they function. Interpreters may be needed to help with the system.

Transportation

Refugees will immediately need transportation from their point of arrival to their new home. Once established, refugees will need transportation to take care of the other physical needs listed here, as well as many of the other needs that are impossible to anticipate. Congregations can prepare for transportation needs by arranging for dependable people to donate time, vehicles, and money for fuel and maintenance. In our mobile society, transportation has become a basic physical need.

Emotional Needs

Like most congregations involved with refugee ministry, the Antelope Park Church discovered that the need for human love and friendship was essential for the Khmer who came to them.

"Maybe the most important thing the families needed was friendship from an American family," said JoEva Jones, a former member of Antelope Park who was actively involved in the early stages of the Khmer ministry. "Refugees need first to feel wanted and loved," she commented.[3]

Naomi Fast, another member involved with the refugees, elaborated. "Somehow the message that we care and love should be uppermost. The image of a generous 'big brother' who knows all, gives all, and has never suffered should be avoided."[4]

Congregations preparing for the emotional needs of an arriving refugee or family need to draw on spiritual resources to offer love and care. Earl Harris, extensively involved in Antelope Park's ministry, reflected, "What is so important to meet the special needs is the love God has placed in us—which is to be freely shared with our brothers and sisters."

Refugees arrive with a mix of fear, pain, love, hope, sorrow, and joy. Human love and personal care are needed in large supply. For churches, these expressions of compassion become the channels through which divine love and care are communicated.

At the entry level, especially when language difficulties prohibit extensive conversation, very basic communication of emotional support is vital. Hugs, smiles, handshakes, and gestures of care communicate far more effectively than words. Just as babies have only limited verbal skills but respond to love in other expressions, so refugees who speak well their own language but know little

English can respond to basic human gestures of love.

Congregations need to find out if there are gestures in the culture of newly arrived refugees particularly appropriate for expressing welcome and friendship, as gestures have varying meanings in different cultures. This should not discourage members from sharing gestures of friendship appropriate in their own culture, however. The tone of voice can also express love, even when the words are not understood.

Congregations can plan for person-to-person or family-to-family support and friendship. They should begin as soon as possible. When Antelope Park Church implemented such a program, its success varied on both the American and Khmer sides. Success of a family-to-family program cannot always be judged on the basis of the initial paired relationship—although initial success is obviously desirable.

Personal relationships help build the bridge between differing cultures and languages. Through these relationships, human love and God's love begin to fill the emotional needs of people in a strange new land.

Psychological Needs

Refugees usually arrive out of traumatic situations. Those interned in refugee camps prior to arrival almost always have suffered psychological trauma. They may have undergone one or more near-death experiences; fear of death and/or torture; extreme hunger, exposure, sickness; and loss of family, friends, and homeland.

The Khmer at Antelope Park have documented such trauma through their painful stories. The struggle to reach safety mixed with the shock of adapting to a new culture add to the trauma. These experiences and emotions create complex psychological and emotional needs.

Listening with interest to stories and memories refugees tell, even if no words are understood, can begin to heal refugee wounds. Congregations and members can prepare to listen by learning any information available about the refugees' personal history from the sponsoring agency. Knowing what caused them to leave their homeland and what kind of journey brought them to their new home can help members listen more caringly. Such information, however, should never take the place of listening to the story in the refugee's own words.

Members of a congregation can offer help without needing specialized study or training in psychology. However, no congregation should substitute lay care for professional psychological or psychiatric care when needed.

Community Needs

Refugees, like all people, need relationships that connect them to people who share their kinship, culture, and heritage. This kinship need is particularly acute for refugees, who have often been wrenched from their culture and heritage.

For this reason, links with people from their native culture, in addition to caring, supportive networks in the new environment, soften the shock of adjusting to the new surroundings. Finding in a present situation a connection with a positive influence from the past culture gives added security for making new connections with new people and a new culture.

A parallel example can be found in the historical patterns of immigration and settlement of people in the Anabaptist heritage who have often been religious refugees. In the United States alone, Brethren and Mennonites often settled in close geographical proximity to one another. Support for refugees to maintain former cultural identities is important, even as they adjust to life in a new place and situation.

Cultural and Linguistic Needs

Congregations often assume that the most important step in preparing for refugee ministry is learning as much as possible about the home country of refugees. However, a new sense of openness must accompany any such learnings. If the change of cultures is a shock for arriving refugees, the refugees' culture is also a shock for the support people who welcome them. Preparing to receive refugees requires as much willingness to experience refugee culture as hosts expect from new arrivals adjusting to the host culture.

Naomi Fast suggested, "Emphasize, encourage, promote in every way possible their music, dance, holidays, family stories, crafts, folk tales, religious customs, work skills. We could learn from them and with them about their geography, political background, agriculture." Reading and studying about the refugees' culture is helpful. But there is no substitute for an openness to the people, their stories, and all that makes them unique.

The best tool for understanding any culture is its language. One member at Antelope Park, Dianne Epp, highlighted the linkage of language with cultural needs.

I think that this [retaining cultural identity] is a critical issue. It is related to language again, and to the way in which Khmer function culturally, which is different from the way in which Anglos function.

Integration was a very big concept in the early days of the refugee ministry in this church. Some felt that all the programs had to be integrated or we somehow would be racist. Not only did this not work for both groups (the church school situation was really frustrating for both Khmer and Anglo students—to say nothing of the teachers). I think it was also damaging to the Khmer in terms of retaining cultural identity.

If one looks historically at refugee groups which have come to the United States, it is clear that in certain areas they have kept using their native language longer than in others. While English may be spoken for everyday contacts, such as work and school, religious services have often been in the native tongue for years after they have become English speakers.

Religion and language are tied together in cultural identity. Provision for worship and study in Khmer would be a healthier pattern in terms of cultural identity.

Learning the language of the arriving refugees, or at least significant phrases, may be the best preparation a congregation can make for refugee ministry. That process will immediately demonstrate the difficulties the refugees will face. Finding interpreters and persons to teach English is an important preparation. Sometimes state refugee offices can provide help with these resources or direct people to them.

English instruction should begin as soon as possible. Some refugees may be unable to read and write their own language. This doubly complicates cultural and language needs. They will need to learn to read and write their own language, as well as a foreign one.

Learning English, however, is no reason to eliminate the native language. Adults will most likely retain skill in their first language. Children in refugee families should learn that their family's native language is valuable and an important part of their heritage. Fluency in the native language will not be a need upon entering a new country. At that point, learning the new language is more critical—but an entry need is to preserve the value of the family's native language.

An example from the Anabaptist heritage helps illustrate. Three hundred years after the first Mennonites arrived in the United States, there are still places where German is spoken daily. Today, many years after the immigrations of the 1700s, some congregations still hold worship services in German. The German language has made a contribution to the cultural and even spiritual heritage of the various bodies tracing their roots to the Anabaptist movement.

Ethnicity and native language in these traditions can be barriers, of course. But they have also made an enriching contribution to the spiritual life of these groups and to the countries where they have made their homes. Refugees must be encouraged to learn the new language while preserving native language and culture.

Spiritual Needs

A failure of modern Christianity in the Western world is viewing spiritual needs as different and separate from other human needs. By keeping spiritual needs distinct from basic human needs, we lose sight of the spiritual value and growth that arise from treating physical needs as expressions of spiritual ministry.

The notion persists that some basic needs, particularly physical needs, must be met first—after which people can learn about Christian faith. Some Christians suggest that providing for physical needs is the highest expression of spiritual care. The other extreme is to center on conversion, with the meeting of other human needs being viewed as ways to stir conversion.

A common current expression of Anabaptist-Pietist traditions is emphasis on service to neighbor as opposed to more individualistic, spiritual expressions of faith. Remembering the Anabaptist-Pietist tradition, the Antelope Park Church tried to maintain a balance between inner growth and outer expression of faith in its refugee ministry.

Ministry to refugees offers Christians an opportunity to see spiritual needs from a much wider perspective than a privatistic, Western Christianity. The refugee experience embedded in the Anabaptist-Pietist heritage can help its current adherents respond with empathy to any and all needs of newly arrived refugees, both physical and spiritual.

All Christians retell the good news about Jesus Christ and practice the teachings of the gospel when they provide for basic physical needs (Matt. 25:31-46). In providing love and care, Christians remember the one who first loved us. Christian faith and teaching intertwine with Christian actions. The two are not exclusive. Meeting spiritual needs should not be delayed and separated from meeting physical, emotional, psychological, community, or cultural needs.

Preparing for spiritual needs can include having Bibles in the language of the arriving refugees. Bibles are available through the American Bible Society and sometimes from denominational offices and other groups.

Preparations can also include planning Sunday school lessons and worship services in English as well as the refugees' language. Refugee ministry may be the expression of faith that helps Western Christians find their way back to a faith that integrates spiritual concerns into every aspect of living. Churches of the Anabaptist tradition have tried to make faith apply to every dimension of our living. Refugee ministry may be a calling for which Anabaptists may be uniquely prepared, and uniquely able to prepare others.

6

And You Included Me: Assimilation

The initial phase of refugee ministry is dominated by the first shocks of differing cultures, finding refuge, and meeting new, often quite different, people. The entry phase may be at times almost euphoric—but also chaotic—for welcoming congregations. The refugee(s) may feel an initial relief brought about by finally realizing the dream of escaping danger. They may also feel over-whelmed by the complexities of their new situation.

As refugees and congregations begin to work through entering a new place and way of life, the initial needs, responses, and emotions change. They may not subside in intensity, but they take on a different shape. No longer is daily survival such an urgent task.

The needs of the refugee in the assimilation process are more complex than those of the entry stage. After the initial entry phase, both refugees and welcoming church members begin to seek ways to feel at home with each other. Refugees may try to find ways to settle into life in a new place while retaining the familiar life of the past. The congregation will begin adjusting to having people from a different setting as part of their life.

Sometimes the adjustment is neglected. By forgetting about the refugees and their needs, some people try to ignore the differences in cultures. Others stay committed, but may find it either harder or more frustrating to meet more complex needs. This is due partly to the changing nature of some of the needs as refugee and congregation try to adjust to and build a relationship with each other. Awareness of the changing needs of refugees as they settle in can help churches and refugees strengthen connections with each other.

Physical Needs

Physical needs still exist during the assimilation stage even though they may not be as urgent as during entry. Likewise, the ways supportive people respond to them must also change as appropriate. Teaching the refugees how they can provide for their own physical needs supersedes actual provision of needs.

The shift in focus is perhaps most visible with physical needs. While this shift does not imply a pulling back by the welcoming church, the temptation to do so can cause deterioration in the congregation's involvement with the refugees. When properly managed, however, shifting to helping the refugees provide for themselves and others can help them as well as church members sense a deeper bond of shared fellowship and living.

Housing

The quality and safety of housing still needs to be monitored. If the initial shelter was inadequate, more suitable housing must be secured. As refugees find employment, they can begin to assume the cost of housing. They may take up tasks related to daily living, such as paying utilities and making simple repairs. The new residents can arrange their living space to give it their personality.

Food

As refugees begin to buy (and perhaps raise) their own food, they may feel less dependent on others. Maintaining traditional dishes and patterns of eating can help preserve their own culture in the midst of a new one.

Some attention to nutritional balance may be needed. More important, food can become an avenue of continuing fellowship long after the initial need to provide food has passed. By sharing meals, people in the congregation can receive from the refugees as well as give. People from different cultures can learn about each other by eating their favorite foods.

Clothing

Some refugees have no distinctive dress when they arrive. Others who arrive in traditional clothing may give it up as they adjust to new surroundings. Traditional clothes may be reserved for use inside the home or for special family occasions. During the period of assimilation, traditional clothing (like food) can provide a link with refugees' cultural heritage, even if some of that clothing is not as functional in the new climate. By valuing traditional dress, congregational members can affirm the native culture of their new friends.

Adequate clothing for climate, work environment, and school are still important. Learning about clothing items, sizes, and places to purchase clothes will help refugees take on more responsibility.

Medical Care

The supporting congregation may need to continue providing for medical care, even during the time of assimilation. Costs and insurance paperwork related to medical care may still require assistance from the congregation.

However, refugees can begin to learn what resources are available—such as health care assistance and locations of doctors, dentists, hospitals, and medical services. Refugees may need to change personal hygiene practices or learn them from scratch. Sponsor congregations need to teach the skills for independence. Refugees of childbearing age may also need help meeting gynecological and obstetrical needs.

Employment

Adjusting to work and the work environment is part of adjusting to a new culture. Supportive congregations should keep in touch with job situations to avoid abusive or exploitative employers or supervisors. As language and other skills improve, better employment opportunities may be possible.

Stewardship and financial management can become new areas of learning. Many North Americans could learn much about their own stewardship and financial management from refugee families who survive on wages their hosts would consider impossibly low.

Working with the System

Congregational members can continue to assist with bureaucratic concerns. As refugees begin to learn English, they can answer more questions on their own. This allows them to do more of their own paperwork. Many governmental refugee offices can offer translators to help. During the time of assimilation, refugees can work toward needing less assistance in bureaucratic matters.

Transportation
In areas where public transportation is available, refugees can begin to provide themselves with transportation before they drive cars. North America's highly mobile society presents a cultural challenge to most refugees. Challenges will likely include learning to drive, obtaining a driver's license, and registering and insuring an automobile. As supporting congregations help refugees with these tasks, refugees continue to increase in their ability to provide for their own needs.

Emotional Needs
Meeting emotional needs remains a high priority during the assimilation period. After the initial shock of entering a different, often strange, culture, the needs for love and human support remain great. This need for human love is even greater for refugees or family units who arrive alone without relatives or companions.

An initial surge of energy and care may burst from the congregation, or at least the most interested members, to cushion the shock of entering a new culture. But the need for committed human love continues beyond arrival. Compassion, love, and friendship expressed in visible, personal ways undergirds the assimilation process. As a congregation expresses love, it in turn receives the love of new friends. Refugees continue to need that love to make the transition to living in a new culture.

Refugee Sokhum Oum expressed this when he said to

the Antelope Park members at an appreciation service, "We share praises to God who brought this about. We offer our appreciation to all of you for reaching out in love to a people you didn't have any reason to love, other than Christ in your hearts."[1]

Refugees need the anchors of human care. In turn, congregations need that love to make the transition to a new, multicultural body that grows through giving and receiving love. Emotional needs are mutual throughout refugee ministry, but especially so in the assimilation phase.

The Antelope Park Church immediately perceived the need for emotional support among the Khmers who arrived in Lincoln. After the initial perception of that need, Naomi Fast worked with Vanna Pel to match interested North American and Cambodian families and individuals. As Naomi wrote in introducing a family-to-family program to the congregation, the period of "simply getting acquainted" was over. It was time to "deepen our relationships, to experience some of the more meaningful relationships."[2]

The family-to-family program set as its initial goal two visits per month between Khmers and church members. Simple activities—such as playing a game, baking cookies, or making a shopping trip to a nearby store—were encouraged.

Success of the family-to-family program varied. Yet the program was a giant step toward meeting the emotional needs of the refugees and congregational members.

Psychological Needs

The shock of sheer survival begins to diminish as refugees settle into their new communities. However, the trauma of the refugee experience may remain locked in silence as refugees are assimilated into their new settings. Telling the stories of their journeys can help refugees through the trauma of adjustment. Congregational listening, even to repeated tellings of the same stories, is an important way to help refugees resolve the past.

During this time, adult refugees may be reluctant to tell their experiences to their children or a younger generation. They may think that keeping silent about the pain of the past will shield their children from the hurt. However, keeping silent may intensify the pain for the adults. Silence may also deny the children of refugees the opportunity to appreciate and respect the survival abilities of their parents. To move beyond the past, while not forgetting or repressing it, refugees need opportunities to share their experiences with younger generations.

During assimilation, the shock of adjusting to a new culture may not be as acute as at the point of entry. But it certainly still exists. Even as refugees try to adjust to a new culture, its differences can generate tension, particularly when the new culture is markedly different from the old. Helpful friends from the welcoming congregation can continue to interpret life in the new culture.

Perhaps the greatest danger during assimilation is to assume that, once refugees have established themselves in their new setting, they are at peace. The outward appearance of being comfortable with new surroundings and taking on the tasks of daily life does not guarantee inner healing from pain in the past.

In some cases, when cultural change is not too intense or when the flight of the refugee is less dangerous, assimilation may take place rapidly. But silence does not insure that a healthy adjustment is taking place. The refugee's need to be heard and included is just as important in adjusting to a new culture as it was upon entry.

Community Needs

As refugees begin to make a home in a new culture, they may begin to make new friends and relationships in that culture. Some may not feel a need to relate as closely to other refugees or people of their ethnic background once they start assimilating. In fact, some may be so eager to assimilate that they completely or partially reject their own heritage and culture. They may try to become as much like their new neighbors as possible.

Ties to a new culture and loyalty to an old one can create complications in the lives of refugees. Assimilation requires a certain openness to the new culture. But roots in the native culture can give refugees strength for dealing with the new one. Otherwise there is danger of quick rejection of the past and false adoption of a new identity. This may hinder a healthy assimilation which affirms both the old and new.

Ties to members of both communities are important for healthy assimilation. Where possible, family relationships and friendships with others in the same ethnic heritage will help ground the refugees in their past identity.

Significant friendships with people in the new culture can help refugees feel a part of a new community without threatening the loss of the old community and identity. Beginning new relationships, as well as strengthening established ones in both original and welcoming communities, eases the confusion caused by the refugee's changing sense of personal and corporate identity.

Churches should provide continuing opportunities for making friends with refugees and strengthening existing bonds. Members of congregations will do well not to expect refugees to become "just like us." High expectations that refugees discard their native cultures add to rather than ease the pain of crossing cultures.

But refugees do need to survive in the new culture. That becomes easier as refugees feel settled in the new environment. Significant caring relationships can help refugees feel a sense of acceptance into communities that are different, yet not separate or closed.

Cultural and Linguistic Needs

Cultural needs are related to community needs during assimilation. Cultures are mixing just as communities mix. The need for the original ethnic culture and identity to coexist with the new culture exists in communities as well. A healthy assimilation happens when a sense of connectedness to both cultures develops.

The period of assimilation is *not* the time to exclude expressions of the original ethnic culture. This is precisely the phase in which to begin planning events and opportunities for celebrating the ethnic culture refugees bring with them. Otherwise, the cultural identity may be in danger of being lost completely. Sensitivity is important here. Do not plan other events on the occasion of important cultural holidays.

The cultural identity of the Khmer was not lost among the refugees in Lincoln, Nebraska.

When the Khmers were casting about for a way to be givers as well as receivers at Antelope Park, Sam Nang [Soch] encouraged the young people to revive their dancing. Chamnan [In] and Bopha [Soy] became excited by the idea. Together they organized and coached a dance troupe of twelve people, ranging in age from eight to twenty-four.

A repertoire of about a dozen traditional Cambodian dances was perfected.[3]

Assimilation is a phase of adjustment. It need not be a phase of surrender. Life in a new culture will bring changes to refugees. Many will learn new skills. They will be confronted by different behaviors, different values, different environmental factors.

Adjusting to the differences is necessary to establish a new home. But adjusting does not require rejection of all they have brought with them. Many values will still be important and even enhance the new culture. Some customs can easily be retained to help remind refugees of their origins, even while they are becoming comfortable in a new home. In Lincoln, Bopha Soy remembered,

> My father had been killed and our family scattered. We did not know who had survived and who had not. In the refugee camp, my mother encouraged me to dance. "Learn our people's traditional dances," she said. "They will help to keep us united, to remember our heritage."[4]

Likewise a welcoming congregation can be enriched as new cultural dimensions are introduced to its body. Dances, songs, food, clothes, values, and many other aspects of the new people can broaden the congregation's appreciation of the diversity of God's creation and people.

During assimilation, refugees will increase their proficiency in English. This may be the time some members of the refugee community drop their native language. Some members of the community who do not learn the language of the welcoming culture may be viewed with less esteem by church members for not using the new language.

Again, assimilation need not mean surrender. The words, stories, and proverbs of a language express its culture. Whether or not the language is written, it is a means of communication and expression of identity. Refugees may feel self-conscious for retaining their original language in a new setting. It may, however, offer an "inside" mode of communication beyond the reach of the new culture.

Congregations, in addition to teaching English, can encourage refugees to teach their native language to refugee children and children (and adults) of the church. During this phase, congregations can try learning simple songs or phrases in the language of refugees as a signal that their culture is, through its language, still valued. Refugees and welcoming congregations can pass more easily into a world of two cultures if expressions of both, including languages, abound side by side.

Spiritual Needs
Spiritual needs are significant during assimilation. Spiritual energy is needed to find comfort for the losses of the past, to encourage retention of the original identity and culture, and to give hope for emerging paths into a new future.

The welcoming congregation can share the Christian faith by participating in refugee ministry, teaching the story of Jesus Christ, and sharing their own spiritual journeys. Congregations must be reminded to impart their faith rather than merely to teach their culture.

Some of the cultural values of the refugees may be closer to the biblical values of Christianity than the values of the host culture. For example, many Eastern cultures value the connectedness of family and respect the aged members of the extended family. In contemporary Western culture and much of Western Christianity, however, personal independence is valued above interdependence of an extended family.[5] In the West, youth is coveted, whereas the elderly are viewed as non-contributing members of society, perhaps even weak and foolish.

These Western values are not found in the Bible. In the Old Testament, the wisdom of the elderly was prized. Older persons were the esteemed teachers of Israel. In the New Testament, naming fellow Christians "brother" and "sister," the exhortations to love, and such inclusive statements as Galatians 3:28 show that early Christians saw faith in Christ as creating an even larger extended family.

Congregations welcoming refugees may find that their new friends minister to them and teach them new lessons about old biblical values. And refugees who have to survive with little can teach North Americans a needed lesson on living happily with less. The danger of North Americans teaching materialism along with faith is an example of confusing culture with faith.

Refugee ministry at its best, then, is mutual. The good news of Jesus Christ, who was himself a refugee and blessed those who welcomed foreigners, is a spiritual gift to share. Refugees can help North American Christians discover a fresh encounter with biblical faith through the experiences of a new culture. At that point, refugee ministry is good news from the refugees for the welcoming congregation. Finding ways of faith that are enriched by differing cultures clears a path for refugees and congregations to walk together on the spiritual journey of refugee ministry.

7

No Longer Strangers and Sojourners: Accommodation

A third phase of refugee experience is accommodation. Refugees are no longer new arrivals seeking shelter. They are becoming neighbors, friends, even citizens in their new home. The new life that began upon their arrival in a new culture is taking shape and becoming part of their identity.

Accommodation may begin a few months after entry. Some refugees may never begin to accommodate to their new culture. Others may not live long enough after arriving in a new home to begin accommodation. Many factors influence when accommodation begins and at what speed it takes place. They include age, health, proximity to other refugees, ministry (or lack of it) from the welcoming community, and individual openness to a new culture.

Degrees of accommodation vary. Some refugees open up to the new culture only with great reluctance. Others try quickly to discard the culture of origin and to become as much like the new environment and people as possible. Most refugees accommodate somewhere between these extremes.

During accommodation, needs are different than they were upon arrival and during assimilation. At this stage, the refugees will be most able to minister to the congregation. During accommodation, the initial clash of cultures at the entry level is past, although differences may persist. The strains of adjustment may be lessening. As refugees and their welcoming congregation become increasingly familiar and comfortable with each other, however, some needs remain.

Physical Needs
Housing and Clothing
The immediate needs of arriving refugees for shelter, food, and clothing have been met by the time of accommodation. Although refugees and their families still need homes, food, and clothing, by the time they become settled in a new community, they are learning ways to provide for those needs themselves, although help may still be required.

Food
Food in particular may no longer be an urgent need. Food may remain an important way to express the original culture. Piquant pepper, aromatic curries, pungent ginger, and bold garlic along with other flavors pass on the heritage of refugees and immigrants. Sharing those foods with church members can become a way of rejoicing in the old culture in the midst of a new culture. Bok choy, injira, dahl, enchiladas, and borsch along with many other foreign foods show that cultures can be experienced by taste as much as by speech.

Medical Care

Medical and dental care will remain a need for refugees after becoming more established. Maintenance of good health care practices and teaching those practices to children is the primary medical need during accommodation. Occasional help with hospitals or with insurance may be needed. However, as refugees become more independent, they may attend to this need for themselves.

Employment

By the time of accommodation, refugees who are able to work will likely have found and become established in a job. Skill levels and English proficiency may have increased, allowing access to jobs with better hours, improved working conditions, or higher wages. Familiarity in the work place brings more ease in dealing with the details of holding a job.

Some refugees will advance in their careers. Others, as they become established in occupations, will become trusted members of the work force. Still others may launch business ventures or pursue scholarly work. The refugee can help others in the ethnic group find employment—thus becoming a vital member of the refugee ministry network.

Job discrimination can be a problem for refugees, as it has been for many members of minority groups.[1] In some places agencies help with the employment search, but finding desirable employment may be still difficult. Church members who work with refugees, especially members who share with refugees a common employer, can be advocates for fair employment practices.

Churches may need to pay close attention to employment needs long after a job has been found. Accommodation is a phase of refugee ministry that helps the refugee become as much at home as possible in the new country. This includes becoming comfortable in the work place.

Working with the System

If no steps toward citizenship have begun during the assimilation stage, such steps should be taken during accommodation. Making a new life in a new culture brings with it the reality of citizenship in a new society. Accommodating to the new life continues as the temporary life of wandering is replaced by settling into a new home.

Labels like "refugee" and "alien" are no longer appropriate for people being integrated into new networks of relationships. During accommodation refugee status is replaced by citizenship.

Continuation of the tutoring in language and culture begun during assimilation may now help refugees gain the proficiency needed to pass citizenship tests. Tutoring on American history and government can help prepare for this step. Individuals in the congregation may be able to provide such tutoring or to help arrange classes which refugees can take. Some churches may offer classes to help refugees prepare for citizenship. This may be a unique opportunity for a congregation to reconsider citizenship from a faith perspective.

As refugees accommodate to the new culture, they may no longer need most of the support services for which they qualified on arrival. But congregational members still should not assume that refugees now need no assistance. Periodic checking in a friendly, concerned way can determine whether further needs for support from agencies and bureaucracies exist.

Transportation

If learning to drive or using public transportation has not been completed during assimilation, it may take place during accommodation. As refugees become more familiar with travel, they will begin to plan trips to relatives or friends in other communities. Khmer refugees helped by Antelope Park Church were able to move to California upon accommodating to a mobile society. There they found a more familiar climate. The freedom and flexibility that come with providing transportation for themselves signal growing self-sufficiency.

Emotional Needs

While the initial overwhelming emotional needs may lessen after entry and assimilation, many emotional needs remain. There may seem to be more human resources for meeting these needs as refugees make new friends. However, the need for caring relationships and friendships remains important. Friends do not come automatically.

Sometimes churches prematurely lessen their concern after the initial rush of activity and outreach following the arrival of refugees. Yet during accommodation refugees need ongoing support to continue the process of feeling settled and at home. Without the openness of caring people who also desire to receive from the refugees, a feeling of connectedness in the new setting will not develop. Perhaps more than in other phases, during accommodation emotional needs are evident on both sides of the relationship between refugees and congregation.

As refugees' time away from relatives and homeland increases, their emotional needs may also increase. Older relatives or friends die, either in the homeland or the new land; each death reinforces the grief over the loss that relocation entails. Distance or lack of communication further intensifies grief. Emotional support following these deaths is vital.

Similarly, as years in the new country pass, and as younger generations adopt the new culture and lose former language and customs, accommodation will remind the refugees of their cultural losses. Conserving memories and symbols of the old culture is a means of emotional support during accommodation. Understanding and affirmation from new friends can help accommodation move toward an integration that values old and new cultures.

Psychological Needs

Psychological needs related to the trauma of the refugee experience may exist even into the accommodation phase. Persons forced into refugee status by particularly violent or threatening circumstances need continuing care as they work through the trauma. In addition to the continued frequent telling of their story which helped in earlier stages, they may also benefit from professional help.

Community Needs

The process of accommodation blends the tensions of the assimilation periods and moves the refugee into identification with the new community. When accommodation is healthy, the new community is an integration of both old and new.

Strong ties, both to others of similar ethnic background and to members of the welcoming community, help this accommodation take place. Programs that match congregational members with refugee individuals and families can form the foundation for such relationships. Congregations can sponsor events, such as singing, cooking, picnicking, or ethnic festivals, that provide the opportunity for refugees and their new friends to nurture their sense of belonging to each other. As new members join the church community, whether refugee or not, they will need to be brought into the network of relationships that bridge cultures.

The needs of the welcoming congregation may be as great as the needs of the refugees by the time of accommodation. Welcoming refugees and integrating them into the life of the faith community can significantly change the identity of the church community. The risks and unknown factors of change can generate fear and uncertainty.

New people, new languages, new ideas, and new questions will come with refugee ministry. The congregation undertaking refugee ministry will become a new people as they accommodate to those they welcome. Just as the tensions of the Gentile mission brought change to the church in the New Testament, refugee ministry will bring change to the local congregation.

Congregations involved in refugee ministry should remember that the refugees themselves will change as a result of being welcomed by a church. They will be part of a new setting, even if they never fully accommodate. At the same time, they will never be completely without the heritage of their past, even if they try to discard it totally.

Accommodation presents both refugees and congregations with the need to integrate with each other. This raises the threat of changing identities. It also opens the possibility of becoming richer in relationships, cultures, and faith. Trust in the power and grace of God can be a key resource for giving birth to this new identity as a people of faith.

Cultural and Linguistic Needs

The greatest danger that the original ethnic culture will be lost occurs during the time of accommodation. The "great American melting pot" concept fostered the myth that immigrants somehow shed their uniqueness when they stepped ashore. They were thought to put on some generic quality of citizenship and nationality that made them Americans.

In their search for an identity stripped away from them as slaves, African Americans have given North Americans a new appreciation of their ethnic diversity. Alex Haley, in his book *Roots*, helped all North Americans rediscover and affirm their ethnic origins.[2] It is hoped that this can include a new appreciation for the only native cultures of this continent, the Native Americans.

Refugees in modern times, however, are still at risk of losing their cultural heritage, either by their own initiative or by social pressure. The loss of the original language is one major turning point that can signal an erosion of the original culture.

Refugee ministry, when truly a ministry and not just a relief service, will include efforts to affirm, preserve, and cherish the original culture of the refugees. The Khmer culture was affirmed at the Antelope Park Church when the Khmer refugees performed their traditional dances, not only for congregational members but for other groups in the United States. Chamnan In and Bopha Soy recounted the importance of dance.

> "In Cambodia, many Christians were taught to despise their traditional dances, to consider them a form of idol worship," Bopha [Soy] explains.
>
> "But my mother did not agree and urged me to keep dancing. Now I believe God is pleased when I dance. I see dance as a way of praising the true God for loving us and staying with us in our trouble. . . ."
>
> "Dancing is our way of showing our unity, our love for each other, and for God," softly explain refugees Chamnan [In] and Bopha [Soy].[3]

Certainly as refugees move toward accommodation to the new culture, many elements of that different culture will become a part of their lives. Flexibility is crucial. Preserving and affirming the original culture does not require living like museum pieces. It does require sensitivity not to degrade the original culture, as well as willingness to integrate as much of that culture as possible into the new life.

The Antelope Park members helped the Khmer to establish the Kampuchean Community Organization. This group, not only assisted the refugees, but also has worked at helping Cambodians (Kampucheans) preserve and pass on their heritage.

One of the great events among the Cambodians in Lincoln is the Cambodian New Year celebration. This event, held at the Antelope Park Church, draws in more than one hundred Cambodians, including those outside the church congregation. Along with native foods, the April celebration include games and dances from Cambodia. People are encouraged to dress in traditional clothing. Church members are also encouraged to attend and participate.

Events such as this Cambodian festival point the way for refugees to meet cultural and linguistic needs during accommodation in order to fit into their new surroundings.

Spiritual Needs

During accommodation, spiritual needs continue to appear. Refugee ministry challenges congregations, not only to welcome and provide physical needs for new people, but also to share the Christian faith and open themselves to new expressions of their faith.

At Antelope Park Church, Bible study was conducted in the Khmer language. Teachers fluent in Khmer were trained with biblical understandings. Worship included singing in English and Khmer. Dances were a part of the Khmer way of worship, representing a change from the Brethren tradition.

At the same time, many of the Khmer were learning about Christianity for the first time. Some had been exposed to Christian faith in refugee camps but only in a preliminary way. Antelope Park attempted to share faith in Christ. Yet it also tried to be sensitive to a culture that had been nearly destroyed by the refugee experience. Both Antelope Park and the refugees learned that spiritual needs can be expressed through a specific culture—yet transcend any one culture. Former pastor Glenn Frazier remembered that

I became aware of the needs which existed, not because they were not spiritual, but because of the intense pressure of materialism. They had a desire to learn about Christ, and we attempted to create many study and discussion opportunities for teaching.[4]

As the body of faith experiences continuing change of identity due to the influx of refugees, new spiritual and pastoral needs surface. Said Glenn Frazier, "Any major growth brings radical changes which create the need for acceptance and relating to the new." Yet in comments that apply to Christians in general as well as to the Brethren, he went on to point out that

If evangelism is ever going to infect the Brethren, we are going to have a basic attitude change. There just are not enough people out there who are German, with the right last name, white skin, and similar values, to build a growing denomination on.

Attempting to meet spiritual needs in refugee ministry raises fears of changes in identity, power structures, and culture. These fears can motivate members to avoid refugee ministry, shift to other priorities, or even withdraw from the congregation. Yet refugee ministry can be an energizing expression of witness and service in Christ's name for a local congregation.

As congregations practice refugee ministry, they can turn to help other congregations. Glenn Frazier pointed out, "There are many people in the Lincoln Church who are now 'experts' in a field many Christians know little about. This is one measure of spiritual gifts invested in the congregation."

One dimension of spiritual needs during accommodation is the need to share and celebrate what has happened and is happening with others. In this way, the congregation that has ministered to and received ministry from refugees can in turn minister to other congregations. Such ministry faithfully lives out the call to discipleship. It serves others in Christ's name and makes disciples who will be able to serve other refugees or any group. It clarifies in powerful ways the meaning of taking up the cross and following Jesus—who taught that "as you did it to one of the least of these . . . you did it to me." (Matt. 25:40)

Notes

Chapter 1

1. A Cambodian refugee story by Many Kim, Lincoln, Nebraska, rewritten by the authors, August 1990. We thank Many Kim for sharing her personal story even as we assume responsibility for the final editing of the story.

Chapter 2

1. Wendy Chamberlain, "Antelope Park Welcomes 97 Khmer Refugees," *Messenger* 131 (March 1982), p. 6.

2. Alan K. Simpson, Introduction to *American Refugee Policy: Ethical and Religious Reflections* (Minneapolis, Minn.: Published by the Presiding Bishops' Fund for World Relief, The Episcopal Church in collaboration with Winston Press, 1984), p. 86.

3. *Report of Findings: A Survey of Public Attitudes Toward Refugees and Immigrants* (New York: Kane, Parsons, and Associates, April 1984), p. 3.

4. *The United Nations at Forty: A Foundation to Build On* (New York: United Nations, 1985), p. 192.

5. Elie Wiesel, "Who Is a Refugee?" in *American Refugee Policy: Ethical and Religious Reflections* (Minneapolis, Minn.: Published by the Presiding Bishops' Fund for World Relief, The Episcopal Church in collaboration with Winston Press, 1984), p. 17.

6. Gretchen Sousa, "Refugiados," *Sojourners* 17 (February 1988), p. 33.

7. Paul Tabori, "Song of Exile," *The Anatomy of Exile—A Semantic and Historic Study* (London: George G. Harrap and Company, 1972), p. 9.

8. Bruce Grant, *The Boat People: An Age Investigation* (New York: Viking Penguin, Inc., 1979), p. 2.

9. Beverly Raphael, *When Disaster Strikes: How Individuals and Communities Cope with Catastrophe* (New York: Basic Books, Inc., 1986), p. 144.

10. Brent Ashabranner and Melissa Ashabranner, *Into a Strange Land: Unaccompanied Refugee Youth in America* (New York: Dodd, Mead and Company, 1987), pp. 11-12.

11. Terri Meushaw, ed., *Windsor Winds* (New Windsor, Md.: New Windsor Service Center, Spring 1987), p. 3.

12. *Agenda* for Church of the Brethren Parish Leaders, Church of the Brethren General Board, June/July 1987, p. 3.

13. For the ideas in this section, I am indebted to Naomi Fast and William Unrau. Major critique of the material was presented by other congregational group members, including Bonnie Ward, Dianne Epp, and Earl Harris.

Chapter 3

1. Anthony J. Bevilacqua, "An Invocation," in *American Refugee Policy: Ethical and Religious Reflections* (Minneapolis, Minn.: Published by the Presiding Bishops' Fund for World Relief, The Episcopal Church in collaboration with Winston Press, 1986), p. x.

2. Jorge Laura-Braud, "Theological Concerns About the Homeless," *Theological Reflections on Refugees* (Church World Service, National Council of Churches of Christ in the United States), p. 7.

3. Alexander Campbell, *The Covenant Story of the Bible*, revised edition (New York: Pilgrim Press, 1963), p. 37.

4. Martin Noth, *A History of Pentateuchal Traditions*, trans. Bernhard W. Anderson (Englewood Cliffs, N.J.: Prentice Hall, Inc., 1972), pp. 47ff.

5. Joseph Blenkinsopp, "Yahweh and Other Dieties," *Interpretation* 40 (October 1986): 365-366.

6. R. K. Harrison, *Leviticus: An Introduction and Commentary* (Downers Grove, Ill.: InterVarsity Press, 1980), p. 227.

7. John Tenhula, "Approaching a Theological/Biblical Statement on Refugee Concerns," *Theological Reflections on Refugees* (Church World Service, National Council of Churches of Christ in the United States), pp. 17-18.

8. Carnegie Samuel Calian, *For All Your Seasons—Biblical Direction Through Life's Passages* (Atlanta: John Knox Press, 1979), p. 79.

9. Edward J. Brady, "Christ Is Present in the Hungry Poor," *CWS Connections* (August 1984), p. 23.

10. Ann Weems, "The Refugees," *CWS Connections* (February 1985), p. 15.

11. James A. Cogswell, *No Place Left Called Home* (New York: Friendship Press, 1983), p. 10.

12. Paul F. Knitter, *No Other Name? A Critical Survey of Christian Attitudes Toward the World Religions* (Maryknoll, New York: Orbis Books, 1985), p. 11.

13. Charles Keely, in *Working with Refugees*, ed. Peter I. Rose (New York: Center for Migration Studies, 1986), p. 103.

Chapter 4

1. J. Ronald Mummert, "Evaluating a Local Church Refugee Program," unpublished manuscript (Oak Brook: Bethany Theological Seminary, 1988). All quotes from members and former members in this chapter came from interviews and correspondence conducted for the earlier unpublished manuscript.

2. Knitter, p. 70.

3. Langdon Gilkey, *Shantung Compound: The Story of Men and Women Under Pressure* (New York: Harper and Row, 1966), p. 242.

4. "The Story of Eath Oum" of Lincoln, Nebraska, told to Vanna Pel. My thanks to Eath Oum for sharing his personal story—and to Vanna Pel (former Khmer Church Secretary at Antelope Park Church of the Brethren) for helping to translate and for permission to use her name. The authors assume responsibility for the final editing of the story.

5. Philip P. Hallie, *Lest Innocent Blood Be Shed: The Story of the Village of Le*

Chambon and How Goodness Happened There (New York: Harper and Row, 1979), pp. 54-55.

Chapter 5

1. Stephen Grenier, M.D., of Lincoln, Nebraska, interview by author, May 1, 1988.

2. Individual Service Record Form—ISR-82, 5th Rev., Refugee Service Center, Inc., a division of the Lao-Hmong Association of Nebraska, 4831 Dodge St., Suite D., Omaha, Nebraska, p. 1.

3. JoEva Jones of Lincoln, Nebraska, interview by author, September 12, 1988.

4. The subsequent quotes are from interviews by the authors with members of the Antelope Park congregation.

Chapter 6

1. Christopher Keating, "Caring About Khmers," *Messenger* 132 (January 1983), p. 13.

2. Introductory letter by Naomi Fast to members of the Antelope Park Church of the Brethren, Lincoln, Nebraska, bulletin insert, May 23, 1982.

3. Kermon Thomasson, "Chamnan In and Bopha Soy: Unity in Traditional Dancing," *Messenger* 132 (January 1983), p. 2.

4. Ibid.

5. The strong sense of community in the Anabaptist tradition may fit its congregations uniquely for refugee ministry.

In "Brethren Identity and the Unity of the Church," *Brethren Life and Thought* 20 (Autumn 1975), p. 206, Warren Groff (former president of Bethany Theological Seminary, Chicago, Ill.) highlighted the potential contribution of this family-like sense of community that holds true for most Anabaptists.

"The catholicity of the church reminds us that Brethren may be graced with strength as a family without becoming provincial and clannish, or indifferent toward other church families, . . . the catholicity of the church . . . extends beyond the small group of like-minded believers, . . . the other Christian individuals and groups that make up the church universal, until finally our discipleship is measured in relation to what God intends for his whole creation."

Chapter 7

1. Job discrimination and prejudice against refugees is well documented. One source the reader could consult is Harvey Arden, "Troubled Odyssey of Vietnamese Fisherman," *National Geographic* (September 1981), p. 378-395.

Arden writes, "While their old boats saved them, the first boats they bought in the United States led to trouble. A small Vietnamese shrimper . . . passes larger American counterparts in Empire, Louisiana. But the tranquility is deceptive, for local antagonism forced most Vietnamese fishermen to leave Empire" (p. 380).

Arden quotes Vietnamese refugee fisherman Ba Peers: "They [local Louisiana fishermen] say there's not enough shrimp and fish for all. They won't let us dock, won't buy our shrimp. They shoot our boats, make threats, chase us. But where can we go?" (p. 384).

2. See Alex Haley, *Roots*, (Garden City, New York: Doubleday & Company, Inc.). On the book jacket are these words: "But Haley has done more than recapture the history of his own family. As the first black American writer to trace his origins back to their roots, he has told the story of 25,000,000 Americans of African descent. He has rediscovered for an entire people a rich cultural heritage that slavery took away from them, along with their names and their identities. But *Roots* speaks, finally, not just to blacks, or to whites, but to all peoples and all races everywhere, for the story it tells is one of the most eloquent testimonials ever written to the indomitability of the human spirit."

3. Thomasson, p. 2.

4. This and subsequent quotes from Glenn Frazier come from an interview by author, January 4, 1988.

Bibliography

Adams, Daniel J. *Cross-Cultural Theology: Western Reflections in Asia.* Atlanta: John Knox Press, 1987.

Afghanistan: A Portrait—A Guide for Resettling Afghan Refugees. New York: Church World Service, Refugee Information Service.

Agenda for Church of the Brethren Parish Leaders, Church of the Brethren General Board, June/July, 1987.

Allen, Ronald J. *Contemporary Biblical Interpretation for Preaching.* Valley Forge, Pa.: Judson Press, 1984.

Arden, Harvey. "Troubled Odyssey of Vietnamese Fishermen." *National Geographic* 160 (September 1981): 378-395.

Ashabranner, Brent and Melissa. *Into a Strange Land: Unaccompanied Refugee Youth in America.* New York: Dodd, Mead and Company, 1987.

Augsburger, David W. *Pastoral Counseling Across Cultures.* Philadelphia: Westminster Press, 1986.

Bailey, Kenneth E. *Poet & Peasant* and *Through Peasant Eyes: A Literary-Cultural Approach to the Parables of Luke*: 2 vols. in one. Grand Rapids, Mich.: William B. Eerdmans Publishing Company, 1983.

Balda, Wesley D., ed. *Heirs of the Same Promise: Using Acts as a Study Guide for Evangelizing Ethnic America.* Monrovia, Calif.: National Convocation on Evangelizing Ethnic America, Mission Advanced Research and Communication Center, 1984.

Becker, Elizabeth. *When the War Was Over: The Voice of Cambodia's Revolution and Its People.* New York: Simon and Schuster, 1986.

Bernhard, H. Fred. "Hospitality: The Essence of the Church's Life and Witness." Doctor of Ministry Project, Bethany Theological Seminary, Oak Brook, Ill., 1982.

Blenkinsopp, Joseph. "Yahweh and Other Deities." *Interpretation* 40 (October 1986): 365-366.

Brady, Edward J., SJ. "Christ is Present in the Hungry Poor." *CWS Connections* (August 1984): 22-23.

Brown, Robert McAfee. *Unexpected News: Reading the Bible with Third World Eyes.* Philadelphia: Westminster Press, 1984.

Brueggemann, Walter. *Hopeful Imagination: Prophetic Voices in Exile.* Philadelphia: Westminster Press, 1984.

Building Bridges. Report and Recommendation of the Canada-U.S. Church Consultation on Refugee Protection and Safe Haven, Washington, D.C., April 11 and 12, 1985. New York: Produced by the Church World Service Immigration and Refugee Program, 1986.

Calian, Carnegie Samuel. *For All Your Seasons: Biblical Direction Through Life's Passages.* Atlanta: John Knox Press, 1979.

Cambodia: The Land and Its People. 3 Orientation Supplement, Cambodian Series, April 1976. New York: Distributed by Lutheran Immigration and Refugee Service. Revised July 1983.

Chamberlain, Wendy. "Antelope Park Welcomes 97 Khmer Refugees." *Messenger* 131 (March 1982): 6.

Cogswell, James A. *No Place Left Called Home.* New York: Friendship Press, 1983.

Crossan, John Dominic. *The Dark Interval: Towards a Theology of Story.* Niles, Ill.: Argus Communications, 1975.

CWS Connections. Elkhart, Indiana: Church World Service, National Council of the Churches of Christ in the United States.

David, James H. and Woodie W. White. *Racial Transition in the Church.* Nashville: Abingdon, 1980.

Day, Albert Edward. *The Captivating Presence.* Nashville: The Parthenon Press, 1971.

Durnbaugh, Donald F. *The Believers' Church.* Scottdale, Pa.: Herald Press, 1985.

Faus, Nancy Rosenberger. *Singing for Peace.* Carol Stream, Ill.: Hope Publishing, 1986.

Galdamez, Pablo. *Faith of a People: The Story of a Christian Community in El Salvador, 1970-1980.* Translated from the Spanish by Robert R. Barr. Maryknoll, New York: Orbis Books, 1986.

Grant, Bruce. *The Boat People: An Age Investigation.* New York: Viking Penguin, Inc., 1979.

Groff, Warren. "Brethren Identity and the Unity of the Church." *Brethren Life and Thought* 20 (Autumn 1975): 197-208.

Haley, Alex. *Roots.* Garden City, New York: Doubleday & Company, Inc., 1976.

Hiebert, Paul G. *Anthropological Insights for Missionaries.* Grand Rapids, Mich.: Baker Book House, 1985.

Horning, Estella. *Believing and Doing (James).* The Foundation Series for Youth, Year 3, Quarter 1, Unit A. Student Booklet. Elgin, Ill.: The Brethren Press; Nappanee, Ind.: Evangel Press; Newton, Kan.: Faith and Life Press; Scottdale, Pa.: Mennonite Publishing House, 1983.

Keating, Christopher. "Caring About Khmers." *Messenger* 132 (January 1983): 11-13.

Kitagawa, Joseph M., ed. *American Refugee Policy: Ethical and Religious Reflections*. Minneapolis, Minn.: Published by the Presiding Bishops Fund for World Relief, The Episcopal Church in collaboration with Winston Press, 1984.

Koenig, John. *New Testament Hospitality: Partnership with Strangers as Promise and Mission*. Philadelphia: Fortress Press, 1985.

Laura-Braud, Jorge. "Theological Concerns About the Homeless." *Theological Reflections on Refugees*. New York: Church World Service, National Council of Christ in the United States. No date given.

Loescher, Gil and John A. Scanlan. *Calculated Kindness: Refugees and America's Half Open Door, 1945 to the Present*. New York: Free Press, 1986.

Making It On Their Own: From Refugee Sponsorship to Self-Sufficiency. New York: A Survey on Refugee Resettlement conducted by Church World Service Immigration and Refugee Program in collaboration with Calculogic Corporation. No date given.

Martin, Paul H. "Ministry to People in Resettlement." Ray E. Horst, consultant. An unpublished paper. Des Moines, Iowa: Department of Home Ministies, Mennonite Board of Missions, February 1982.

May, Someth. *Cambodia Witness: The Autobiography of Someth May*. Edited by James Fenton. New York: Random House, 1986.

Menshaw, Terri, ed. *Windsor Winds*. New Windsor, Md.: New Windsor Service Center (Spring 1987): 3.

Michael, Christine. "Equipping Congregations for Urban Ministry." Doctor of Ministry Project, Bethany Theological Seminary, Oak Brook, Ill., 1984.

Mummert, J. Ronald. "Evaluating a Local Church Refugee Program." Learning Unit III, Bethany Theological Seminary, Oak Brook, Ill., 1988.

Myers, Ched. "Embracing the Way of Jesus." *Sojourners* (August/September 1987): 27-30.

New Beginnings. Church of the Brethren Newsletter (January 1983): 3.

Norwood, Frederick A. *Strangers and Exiles: A History of Religious Refugees*, Vols. I and II. Nashville: Abingdon Press, 1969.

Noth, Martin. *A History of Pentateuchal Traditions*. Translated by Bernahard W. Anderson. Englewood Cliffs, N.J.: Prentice-Hall, Inc., 1972.

Nouwen, Henri J. M. *Gracias!: A Latin American Journal*. San Francisco: Harper & Row, 1970.

Oum, Eath. "The Story of Eath Oum" as told to Vanna Pel in "Evaluating a Local Church Refugee Program," Doctor of Ministry Learning Unit III by J. Ronald Mummert, 37-39. Bethany Theological Seminary, Oak Brook, Ill., 1988.

Parvin, Earl. *Missions USA*. Chicago: Moody Press, 1985.

Plank, Karl A. "Broken Continuities: 'Night' and 'White Crucifixion.' " *The Christian Century* 104 (4 November 1987): 963-966.

Poling, James N. and Donald E. Miller. *Foundations for a Practical Theology of Ministry*. Nashville: Abingdon Press, 1985.

Raphael, Beverley. *When Disaster Strikes: How Individuals and Communities Cope with Catastrophe*. New York: Basic Books, Inc., 1986.

Refugee/Disaster Update. New Windsor, Md.: New Windsor Service Center Refugee/Disaster Program.

Refugees. Palais des Nations, Geneva, Switzerland: Published monthly by the Public Information Section of the United Nations High Commissioner for Refugees.

Report of Findings: A Survey of Public Attitudes Toward Refugees and Immigrants. Submitted to: United States Committee for Refugees. New York: Kane, Parsons & Associates, April 1984.

Reynolds, Irene S. "Khmakhane Anothysene: Bulletins in Lao." *Messenger* 130 (September 1981): 3.

Roop, Eugene F. *Living the Biblical Story*. Nashville: Abingdon Press, 1979.

Rose, Peter I., ed. *Working with Refugees*. Proceedings of the Simon S. Shargo Memorial Conference. New York: Center for Migration Studies, 1986.

Sappington, Roger E. *Brethren Social Policy 1908-1958*. Elgin, Ill.: The Brethren Press, 1961.

Service News. "Special Focus: Refugees." Vol. 33. Elkhart, Ind.: Church World Service, November 1980.

Shawcross, William. *The Quality of Mercy: Cambodia, Holocaust, and Modern Conscience*. New York: Simon and Schuster, 1984.

Sheehy, Gail. *Spirit of Survival*. New York: William Morrow and Company, Inc., 1986.

Shenk, Wilbert, R., ed. *Mission Focus: Current Issues*. Scottdale, Pa.: Herald Press, 1980.

Simpson, Alan K. "United States Refugee Policy and Ethical Principles," in *American Refugee Policy: Ethical and Religious Reflections*. Edited by Joseph M. Kitagawa. Minneapolis, Minn.: Published by the Presiding Bishops Fund for World Relief, the Episcopal Church in collaboration with Winston Press, 1984.

Smith, Aanmae. "Face to Face," in *Face to Face: The Ministry of Refu-*

gee Resettlement. Lutheran Immigration and Refugee Service Workbook for Congregations and Community Groups. New York: Lutheran Council in the United States of America, 1984.

Smyser, W. R. "Refugees: A Never-Ending Story." *Foreign Affairs* 64 (Fall 1985): 154-168.

Song, Choan Seng. *Tell Us Our Names: Story Theology from an Asian Perspective*. Maryknoll, New York: Orbis Books, 1984.

_____. *Third-Eye Theology: Theology in Formation in Asian Settings*. Maryknoll, New York: Orbis Books, 1979.

Sousa, Gretchen. "Refugiados." *Sojourners* 17 (February 1988): 33.

Sweet, Leonard I. "The Rainbow Church." *The Christian Ministry* 17 (March 1986): 5-8.

Szymusiak, Molyda. *The Stones Cry Out: A Cambodian Childhood, 1975-1980*. Translated by Linda Cloverdale. New York: Hill and Wang, 1986.

Tabori, Paul. *The Anatomy of Exile: A Semantic and Historical Study*. London: George G. Harrap and Company, 1972.

Tenhula, John. "Approaching a Theological/Biblical Statement on Refugee Concerns." *Theological Reflections on Refugees*. New York: Church World Service, National Council of the Churches of Christ in the United States, Overseas Ministries Immigration and Refugee Program. No date given.

Thomasson, Kermon. "Chamnan In and Bopha Soy: Unity in Traditional Dancing." *Messenger* 132 (January 1983): 2.

Trible, Phyllis. *Texts of Terror: Literary-Feminist Readings of Biblical Narratives*. Philadelphia: Fortress Press, 1984.

Tripp, Rosemary E., ed. *Cambodian Refugees in Thailand: The Limits of Asylum*. New York: United States Committee for Refugees, August 1982.

Underwood, Nora. "Era of the Homeless." *Maclean's* 25 (August 1986): 16.

United Nations at Forty: A Foundation to Build On. New York: United Nations, 1985.

Wagner, C. Peter. "A Vision for Evangelizing the Real America." An unpublished plenary session address, Monday evening, April 15, 1985, at National Convocation on Evangelizing Ethnic America, Houston, Texas, 1985.

Webber, George W. *Today's Church: A Community of Exiles and Pilgrims*. Nashville: Abingdon Press, 1979.

White, Peter T. "Kampuchea Wakens from a Nightmare." *National Geographic* 161 (May 1982): 590-623.

Wiesel, Elie. "Who Is a Refugee?" in *American Refugee Policy: Ethical and Religious Reflections.* Edited by Joseph M. Kitagawa. Minneapolis, Minn.: Published by the Presiding Bishops' Fund for World Relief, The Episcopal Church in collaboration with Winston Press, 1984.

Windsor Winds. New Windsor, Md.: New Windsor Service Center.

World Refugee Survey, 1986, in Review. Washington, D.C.: U.S. Committee for Refugees, 1986.

Yoder, John Howard. *The Politics of Jesus.* Grand Rapids, Mich.: Eerdmans, 1972.

The Authors

J. Ronald Mummert is pastor of the North Liberty (Indiana) Church of the Brethren. He was pastor of the Antelope Park Church of the Brethren (Lincoln, Neb.) for five years. He has served pastorates in Pennsylvania, Ohio, and Iowa for over twenty years.

Originally from York, Pennsylvania, he received his A.B. degree in Bible and philosophy from Elizabethtown College (Pa.); his M. Div. from Bethany Theological Seminary (Ill.); his M.Ed. from Miami University (Ohio); and his doctorate in refugee ministry from Bethany Theological Seminary.

Mummert is married to Constance Louise Sorrell from Middletown, Ohio. They have one son, Shawn.

Jeff Bach served as pastor of a rural congregation of the Church of the Brethren in Prairie City, Iowa. The Prairie City Church was involved in refugee ministry following World War II, again in 1980, and most recently with another family in 1989.

Bach is a graduate of McPherson College and Bethany Theological Seminary. He has written for the Brethren

Adult Sunday School curriculum, for a denominational study on ministry, and for the Brethren Encyclopedia.

Bach and his wife, Ann, are parents of two daughters, Elizabeth and Rebecca. They enjoy travel, playing in the garden, and making music.

Bach is currently pursuing service to the church through graduate studies, making Durham, North Carolina, the most recent family home.